POLITICAL
EVANGELISM

RICHARD J. MOUW

POLITICAL EVANGELISM

WILLIAM B. EERDMANS PUBLISHING COMPANY
Grand Rapids, Michigan

Library of Congress Cataloging in Publication Data

Mouw, Richard J
    Political evangelism.

    1. Christianity and politics.   2. Social ethics.
I. Title.
BR115.P7M59   261.7   73-16213
ISBN 0-8028-1544-8

Scripture quotations are from the Revised Standard Version
Bible and used by permission.

CONTENTS

PREFACE

This book is, in a sense, a progress report on a personal quest. My training within the environs of "conservative-evangelical" Christianity did not provide me with a theological framework adequate to deal with the concerns over social injustice, racism and militarism that were so much a part of the years I spent doing graduate study at secular universities. Yet it seemed to me then—and the conviction, if anything, has gotten stronger in the past few years—that such concerns must be integrated into a larger concern for sound theology and faithful witness, which are integral to the way of Christian discipleship.

Christians must not choose the political passivity that has often been the posture of a culture-denying fundamentalism; nor must they engage in the mindless activism that has regularly characterized the stance of liberal worshipers at the altar of "relevance." These errors can be avoided if political involvement is firmly grounded in submission to the Word of God in obedience to the Lord of the church.

The title of this book indicates my concern to see political action as an aspect of the evangelistic task of the church. This concern is meant to remedy several misunderstandings. First, it may correct the impression given by those who define "evangelistic activity" too

7

narrowly and go on to disparage any form of cultural or political involvement. Second, it may also speak against those who, while also narrowing the scope of evangelism, mean thereby to disparage evangelistic activity. Third, it is meant to provide a corrective to those inclined to approve both "personal evangelism" and political activity, but in a way that the latter is not considered to be as central to the Christian calling as the former.

To speak of "political evangelism" with these concerns in mind is not a mere rhetorical trick. The expression points to the *unity* of the mission of the church in the world, a unity that must be stressed if we are to avoid the imbalance and polarization that continually threaten the Christian community. It is simply a fact that those who have seen it as their calling to invite men to make a personal commitment to Jesus Christ have often denigrated working for political change, and vice versa. This need not be. What follows is an attempt to view both emphases as important aspects of a more comprehensive commitment to evangelism.

Much of the discussion in these chapters reflects my suspicion that the political attitudes of evangelical Christianity have been based on an inadequate theology in the areas of ecclesiology (doctrine of the church) and eschatology (doctrine concerning "last things"). If my suspicion is correct, those evangelicals whose pleas for a more active social and political witness appeal solely or mostly to the Old Testament prophets are missing the central issues with respect to the non-activism of their fellow evangelicals. For this reason I have attempted to present a New Testament case for political evangelism, one which deals explicitly with the relationship between Old Testament Israel and the New Testament church, as well as with the relationship between political witness in "the present age" and the biblical hope of the future return of Jesus Christ as victorious King.

I have also attempted—although probably not with complete success—to keep my discussion free from the tones of accusation and "calls for repentance" sometimes found in discussions by Christians calling their fellow-believers to engage in a "radical Kingdom-witness." The Body of Jesus Christ must be a community where healing and sanctification can take place; and for such an atmosphere to be promoted there must be times when the threat of judgment is set aside so that we can calmly search the Scriptures in order to know better what it is that the Lord requires of us.

During the past ten years, in which many of the thoughts that appear in the following pages were prepared and processed, I have learned much from the words and deeds of such thoughtful Christians as Dietrich Bonhoeffer, Martin Luther King, Daniel Berrigan, and the like. But their contribution to my understanding of the Christian life and witness is small when placed alongside what I have learned from faithful parents, Sunday School teachers, ministers, and evangelists, who, by teaching and example, have urged on me the supreme importance of knowing that one belongs to Jesus Christ. I am now convinced that their vision is one which needs expansion. This book is written in gratitude that the foundation they offered is durable enough to build on.

Some of the thoughts which are presented in this book have appeared elsewhere. Readers of the *Reformed Journal* will recognize themes I have dealt with from time to time in editorials, articles, and reviews in that publication. Parts of Chapter 3 first appeared in my article, "Evangelicals and Political Activism," in the December 27, 1972, *Christian Century*—and are used here with the permission of that magazine.

At one point in this book (Chapter 6) I have felt it necessary to modify a position that I defended earlier in print. In "The Church and Social Specifics" (*Reformed Journal,* July-August 1969) I strongly criticized the view that the church does not have—or rarely has—the authority to take "official stands" on specific social and political matters. I am still inclined basically to agree with my reasoning in that article; but I am less enamored of the positive role that "political sermons" can play in the life of the people of God. This, it should be pointed out, is for me a shift in *tactics,* and not a lessening of my conviction that the Christian community must continually seek the way of political obedience.

Finally, I must thank those who have personally contributed to the process which culminates in the appearance of this book. Discussion with my colleagues both at Calvin College and the *Reformed Journal* concerning issues that I treat in this book, especially the criticisms and insights contributed over the last several years by Peter De Vos, George Marsden, Henry Stob, and Nicholas Wolterstorff, has been invaluable to me. Debate and dialogue in recent months with my fellow board members and the staff of the Grand Rapids Youth Ministry have helped me to get a clearer focus on the issues at stake in finding a framework for Christian evangelism; that involvement has placed me in a special debt to Norman De Graaf, who has taught me many practical lessons concerning the relationship of politics to evangelism. Most of all, I am indebted to my wife, who has contributed to both the letter and the spirit of this book in more ways than she can know, as well as in ways that *only* she can know.

1

THE SCOPE OF
POLITICAL EVANGELISM

"I am the door; if any one enters by me, he will be saved, and will go in and out and find pasture. The thief comes only to steal and kill and destroy; I came that they may have life, and have it abundantly."

John 10:9-10

THE PEOPLE OF GOD are called to engage in the task of evangelism. In fulfilment of this task they must bring a message of good news to a sinful world. This message must be proclaimed in words and demonstrated in deeds. The simplest formulation that can be given to the message is this: "Jesus saves!" The full message of the gospel is implicit in these two words. However, this simple formula can be misunderstood and misused—as it often has been in the past—if two considerations are not kept clearly in mind.

First, we must be clear about what Jesus Christ saves men from. Jesus Christ did not come into the world merely to save men from their anxieties, or their boredom, or their bad habits; he came to rescue the entire created order from the pervasive power of sin. When man first succumbed to the tempter's challenge to "be like God," he involved the entire human race in a radically destructive and disintegrating sinful project that extends its influence throughout the created order. There is no way in which sinners can, by their own efforts, escape the grip of sin. But God in his sovereign mercy has sent his Son into the world to become involved in the agonies of the sinful condition, so that by his death and resurrection he might break the bonds of sin and death. The proclamation that "Jesus saves" is never complete unless it is clearly related to the source of the human predicament, namely, the pervasive power of sin.

Second, we must be clear about what Jesus Christ saves men for. Jesus Christ did not come into the world merely to give men "peace of mind" or to make them "happier" or to help them to be less selfish. He came to provide for the abundant life that comes from living in accordance with God's creative purposes for human beings. This is the life of reconciliation and "wholeness" found by submitting to the full lordship of Jesus Christ. It is misleading to declare that we are simply "saved to tell others" (as the gospel chorus phrases it). The primary aim of Christ's atoning work among men is rather to create a new quality of human life. The desire to witness concerning that new life in Christ to those who have not experienced the healing power of the gospel will of course follow. But the proclamation "Jesus saves" is incomplete until it is clearly related to the building up of the life of reconciliation that salvation brings.

Evangelism, then, must be concerned with the proclamation and demonstration of the full gospel, and with bringing that gospel into confrontation with the pervasive power of sin. The term "personal evangelism" is often used to denote a specific kind of evangelistic activity, but *all* evangelism is "personal," in that all evangelism is directed toward persons and engaged in out of concern for persons.

But evangelistic activity must take place on many fronts, for the gospel in its fulness must be directed to all dimensions of human life. Christ's atoning work offers liberation for people in their cultural endeavors, in their family lives, in their educational pursuits, in their quests for sexual fulfilment, in their desire for physical well-being. It also offers liberation in the building of political institutions and the making of public policy. It is in these latter contexts that we can discuss, in this book, political evangelism.

INDIVIDUALS AND POLITICAL STRUCTURES

Political evangelism, as we shall understand it here, is one aspect of the overall evangelistic task of the people of God. Of course, political evangelism itself has many aspects. For one thing, it involves bringing the gospel to individual persons as we encounter them in the political realm, for no evangelistic activity can be far removed from a concern with broken, sin-torn lives. Thus, political evangelism is concerned to share the Christian message with individual officeholders, with persons experiencing political oppression, and with others who are experiencing the special fears, tensions, and frustrations occasioned by involvement in the political process.

Our thesis, however, is that political evangelism must also be concerned with political structures, processes, and policies. Let us look at some reasons for this.

First, while the sin of the Fall began in the human heart, its influence is not limited to our "private" lives. The sinful project of our first parents very quickly disrupted and distorted family relations, language, technological activity (as in the Tower of Babel episode), and the building of political institutions. As a remedy for the pervasive influence of sin, the redemptive work of Jesus Christ has cosmic implications, and we are called to witness to the radical scope of his reconciling power.

Second, it is wrong to think that all of our social

and political problems will be solved simply by changing individual lives. Somewhere, undoubtedly, there is a Christian slum-dweller who rents from a Christian slum-landlord. Each has experienced the redeeming power of the gospel in a personal way, but the reconciliation they might experience together in Jesus Christ is severely hindered by the kind of social system in which they live. There are economic practices, laws, and prejudices woven into the very fabric of society which make it impossible adequately to deal with the reconciliation of such individuals without at the same time being concerned with the social and political context of their relationship.

Third, in a more general way, the message of the church to individuals cannot be separated effectively from a critical stance toward the general patterns of social and political life. It is not enough to tell a salesman that Jesus Christ can release him from the need to "prove" himself through manipulation, deception, and striving for success. We must also work toward creating an economic environment in which it is possible for him to pursue his vocation as a life of service without needing to resort to telling "half-truths" and blatant falsehoods. We cannot preach a message of nondiscriminating love of neighbor without addressing the problem of discriminatory employment practices. To teach our children that racist attitudes are sinful is empty unless we actively work to create educational systems in which those attitudes are combated.

Fourth, evangelism must be concerned with the whole man. At the very least, a concern for needs other than purely "spiritual" ones is often necessary as preparation for presenting the claims of Christ on a person's life. Christians have usually recognized that it is futile to present the gospel to a starving man without first giving him food, or to a man beset with pain without first bringing him physical relief. But similar preparation is often necessary in relation to social and political matters. The anger and frustration of the victim of racial prejudice or political oppression can often make it practically impossible for him to listen to the Christian message. It is important for Christians to identify with such agonies and to work toward their elimination, not only as a demonstration of the fulness of the gospel's power, but also as a necessary part of creating a meaningful atmosphere for the presentation of that gospel to individuals.

A fifth consideration closely relates to some of the others. Expressions like "national character," "climate of opinion," and "class consciousness" suggest the existence of a reality that cannot be explained as no more than the sum of individual traits or opinions. Without embracing social or economic "determinism" we must nonetheless acknowledge the formative influence of fundamental moods and attitudes perpetrated and reinforced by social practices, the mass media, and ethnic or economic bonds. Preachers and evangelists who have expressed concern over the "moral climate" of the day—usually in relation to such things as sexuality, alcohol, and drugs—have recognized the formative power of general social patterns in at least one area. But we must also stress the influence of general *political* and *economic* "climates." Christians, like the Old Testament prophets, must be concerned with such issues and must acknowledge that they cannot be dealt with adequately in one-to-one relationships. They must also be addressed by means of proclamations in the marketplace and the legislature.

We must return to what we stressed above about

evangelism in general. Like all forms of evangelism political evangelism is in an important sense *personal* evangelism. It is concerned with social and political structures insofar as they affect individual persons. It is motivated by the desire that political processes and policies preserve and promote the dignity of the individuals who bear God's image. It will articulate biblical norms for collective human life. Just as the biblical message speaks to men and women in their roles as fathers, mothers, husbands, wives, church members, consumers, and the like, it also speaks to them in their roles as military strategists, framers of economic policy, political decision-makers, molders of opinion, and voters. To witness to the power of the gospel in these areas is an important aspect of the evangelistic activity of the Body of Jesus Christ.

THE IMPORTANCE OF POLITICAL EVANGELISM

This discussion of political evangelism is meant to counteract two common distortions concerning Christian political activity. First, there are those who would pay too little attention to such activity, either by completely ignoring the need for political witness or by relegating it to a role of legitimate but peripheral concern. We shall deal with this deemphasizing posture in the next chapter and, by implication, throughout the discussion. On the other side are those who would overemphasize the importance of political activity to the detriment of other aspects of Christian life and witness.

These distortions can be avoided only if we view Christian political witness in the light of the fulness of the gospel of Jesus Christ and the total calling of the people of God in the world. It is for this reason that we shall stress the need for a context for evangelism. God's people are called by him to be a faithful community. When we recognize this, we can avoid the error of failing to seek to be a politically obedient community, and we can also avoid the temptation of viewing the Christian life as primarily a matter of political activity.

2

CHRISTIANS AND POLITICS: SOME MISCONCEPTIONS

"God was in Christ reconciling the world to himself, not counting their trespasses against them, and entrusting to us the message of reconciliation. So we are ambassadors for Christ, God making his appeal through us. We beseech you on behalf of Christ, be reconciled to God."

II Corinthians 5:19-20

OUR PURPOSE IN THIS BOOK is to provide a constructive framework for viewing Christian political activity in a positive light—not to argue directly against other possible frameworks. Still, it might be helpful at the outset to deal briefly with some considerations Christians have offered as reasons for *not* taking political activity very seriously. Our comments here will also serve to introduce some of the main points to be developed in the further discussion.

REDEMPTION AND POLITICS

Christians who disparage political activity or rank it low on the list of Christian priorities often do so in words like these: "The redemption of the world doesn't hang on politics." In a sense we must agree with this statement. Most clichés do have an element of truth. But if the redemption of the world does not "hang" on politics, neither does it "hang" on preaching, teaching, personal evangelism, or any other human activity. The redemption of the world "hangs" on the free, sovereign purposes of God, and it will come to pass only when and because God has so chosen.

However, once we raise the question of *how* God has chosen to bring his redemptive purposes to fruition in the world, we can get a proper perspective on

23

human activity in various spheres. God has chosen to call apart a people as the instrument for revealing his Kingdom. Notice two things about this. First, God has chosen to use a *people* as the means for expediting his redemptive purposes: "You are a chosen race, a royal priesthood, a holy nation, God's own people, that you may declare the wonderful deeds of him who called you out of darkness into his marvelous light" (I Peter 2:9). Our communal efforts, our witness to the full triumphs of Christ's atoning work, are the means by which God elects to make his redemptive purposes known among men.

Second, our faithful witness to the triumphs of God's grace must direct men to the coming of God's *Kingdom,* as it will be revealed in its completeness at Christ's return and as it is already present among men. The New Testament's use of the political term "kingdom" to describe the sum of God's redemptive purposes indicates that the total transformation of all things which God intends for his creation includes a transformation of the political realm as well as other realms. The first coming of the Son of Man into the world was not only a challenge to individual sinners and ecclesiastical institutions; it was a threat to the political status quo. It was politicians who sought to kill Jesus shortly after he was born, and it was politicians who finally had a hand in his death.

Christians have too often muted the political message of the gospel by their narrow interpretations of Christ's comments on the political establishment of his day. When Caesar puts his imprint on a coin (cf. Matthew 22:15-22), he does not thereby cancel out God's ownership of the silver and gold, which he has created and which he calls men to use obediently and responsibly. And the politician to whom Christ said, "My kingdom is not of this world" (John 18:36) was the same politician whose seal Christ shattered as he burst forth victoriously from the tomb. The early disciples of the risen Lord were persecuted because they gave him a title—"Lord"—that earthly politicians coveted. And in the midst of their tribulations they were comforted by greetings in the name of the one who was not only "the first-born of the dead" but also "the ruler of the kings on earth" (Revelation 1:5).

There are questions about the relationship between the Christian and earthly political authority, questions that, in view of such passages as Romans 13:1-7 and I Peter 2:13-17, cannot be passed over lightly. We shall discuss these matters in detail further on. But this much must be stressed here: the redemptive work of Christ is, among other things, a *political* redemption. His lordship will not be fully manifest until every knee bows and every tongue confesses that lordship; and no political officeholder will be exempt from this submission. To be sure, these things have not yet come to pass. The political realm is not yet subject to the lordship of Christ. But it is precisely because of this that God calls us to testify to the new life that we have in Jesus Christ. Our testimony must be that the new life is also a new *political* life—which is in turn the hope of a political "glory to come."

SPECIFIC PROGRAMS AND GOD'S WILL

A second cliché often used to dispute those who relate Christianity to politics is this: "We ought not to identify our own specific political programs with the will of God." Christians who articulate this sort of prohibition often have in mind a particular situation in which a specific program has mistakenly been iden-

25

tified with the Kingdom of God. There is no denying that mistakes have been made in this area. When Walter Rauschenbusch identified the Kingdom of God with socialism he was on important points wrong. So is the radio preacher who identifies the Kingdom of God with the "American way of life." So are those radical theologians who would identify the Kingdom of God with contemporary revolutionary movements.

But we must admit that mistakes have been common in other areas also. Faulty exegesis of Scripture has been prefaced with "Thus saith the Lord!" Cruel and mindless personal criticisms and false accusations have been leveled in God's name. Questionable projects in finance, evangelism, and missions have been launched with appeals to divine mandate. None of this proves that Christians ought not to seek to be faithful, to struggle to know God's will in these areas. It merely points to the *general* difficulty of knowing God's will with respect to specific matters. The existence of such a difficulty is not a reason for inaction; rather, it demonstrates the need for prayer, careful study of the Scriptures, reflection, and discussion.

To speak and act in the name of the Lord is always a difficult and fearsome thing. To think that we could legitimately do so would be the ultimate pretension were it not for God's announced intention to speak and act through the faithful people he has chosen. The difficulties involved in speaking and acting politically in the name of the Lord are not absent in other areas of Christian life and witness. No responsible minister finds it easy to stand before his congregation full of confidence that his words are the specific words God would have him speak to the peculiar people before him. And how often does an individual Christian present a "Christian witness" to a specific person with the legitimate certainty that he knows the exact thoughts God would have him convey? To speak and act in the name of God in specific situations are always things that ought to be done in fear and trembling. But we can also do so with the knowledge that God has promised to bless the words and deeds of those who seek to be faithful to him.

POLITICS AND ESCHATOLOGY

The third misconception cannot be stated in the form of a single cliché. It is expressed with a number of clichés, or by appealing to certain biblical texts in a way that is similar to quoting clichés. What is common to these clichés and "proof-text" citings is that they relate directly to views concerning the future return of Jesus Christ.

Those who ground their Christian hope in the return of Christ disagree among themselves about the various events relating to his return. These disagreements often stem from differing emphases in biblical interpretation, but they generally center on differing interpretations of the reference in Revelation 20:6-7 to a "thousand-year" reign of Christ on the earth. Premillennialists interpret this as a reference to a literal thousand-year period, during which Christ shall rule the earth immediately following his future return. Amillennialists, on the other hand, take this to be a symbol of the victorious establishment of the Kingdom of God, which came about as a result of the death and resurrection of Jesus Christ. This Kingdom will be revealed in its full perfection only when Christ returns, but, the amillennialists believe, it is present now and its power can be seen in partial and fragmentary ways. A third school, postmillennialism, which is not very popular today, expected the church's influence successfully to pervade the earth during a period that would immediately precede the return of Christ.

Those who are pessimistic about extensive Christian political activity often base that attitude on a belief that very little progress can be made in this area short of the return of Christ. It is not uncommon for Christians to refuse to protest against military exploits on the ground that "there will be no true peace until the Prince of Peace returns," or to refrain from speaking out against poverty because "the poor we shall always have with us," or to adopt an attitude of resignation toward human conflict since "there will be wars and rumors of wars in the last days."

In order to see that such justifications for political inactivity are inadequate we need not settle the major issues debated by the three schools described above. Clearly amillennialism and postmillennialism provide a basis for Christian political activity. But what of premillennialism? Let us, for the sake of the argument, set forth a rather extreme version of premillennialism, and then look at the consequences of that view for Christian political activity. Let us assume for the moment that the meaning of what the Bible says about the Lord's return is that no lasting solutions to the problems of war, poverty, and racial strife can be realized until Christ comes again to earth, and that indeed there will be an increase in the scope of such tensions just before the Kingdom is miraculously ushered in.

Now, what follows if we hold such a view of these things? For one thing, even if we are convinced that political activity would be out of place in the "last days," we cannot be justified in ignoring the political situation unless we are *certain* that we are in fact living in that period which will immediately precede the return of Christ. Legitimate certainty about such things is not easy to come by, since there have been past periods that have known many of the conditions we observe today. Moreover, the Scriptures do not permit us to think that there is ever a time when a concern for the poor and oppressed is simply out of place. As Vernon Grounds, a premillennialist, has written:

> The Church must keep reminding us that God has his own program mapped out for changing the world by the personal intervention of Jesus Christ, who will return to establish the Kingdom of heaven on earth. Yet simultaneously the Church must keep reminding us that there is no biblical reason for concluding that enormous evils cannot be significantly changed before our Lord comes back. The Church, consequently, must keep reminding us as New Testament believers that, whatever our political alignment, we ought to be spiritual subversives, duplicating the redemptive radicalism of those first-century Christians who were condemned for turning the world upside-down. The Church must keep reminding us that we are God's saboteurs working to bring about a revolution of faith and hope and love ("Bombs or Bibles? Get Ready for Revolution!", *Christianity Today*, January 15, 1971, p. 6).

In reflecting on the relationship between our political activity and the return of Christ we must also be clear about the requirements of the divine mandate to which our Christian witness is a response. The Christian is not called to launch programs that are successful in terms of human criteria. The Christian is called to be faithful to the heavenly vision. Thus, even if we could be certain that we live in an age in which the smallest degree of political success is impossible, this would in no way cancel our obligation to witness faithfully to the full triumphs of Christ's atoning work. When Christ returns he will be concerned to find us faithful in living out the demands of discipleship. A conviction that his return is not far off should only reinforce our desire to witness to his power.

ISRAEL AND THE CHURCH

One more misconception should be mentioned here, though a full discussion of the issues involved is undertaken in Chapter 3. Christian political activity is often disparaged on the basis of a rigid distinction between the political messages of the Old and New Testaments. The argument goes like this: the majority of biblical passages that have to do with social and political issues are in the Old Testament. There we find God calling a nation into being—a nation that has a very special relationship with him. Israel was basically a "theocracy," and it was thus quite proper for the Old Testament prophets to speak to the issues of government, war, poverty, economics, and the like. But Christians in the New Testament era are living under secular governments. Therefore, their relationship to government is of a different sort from that of the Old Testament prophets to Israel. The New Testament does speak about some social issues—for example, the plight of the poor is discussed in the Epistle of James—but the stress here is on performing individual acts of charity, not on speaking out on issues of political policy.

To see the confusion of this line of argument, let us consider a specific example. Both Old Testament Israel and modern nations have often been guilty of the sin of national pride. Whenever Israel blinded itself to the will of God and pursued its own selfish policies through corruption and exploitation, there was a call to return to the way of faithfulness. The means for becoming a faithful nation are clearly outlined in God's promise to Solomon recorded in II Chronicles 7:14: "If my people who are called by my name humble themselves, and pray and seek my face, and turn from their wicked ways, then I will hear from heaven, and will forgive their sin and heal their land."

Now, suppose that a modern nation were to pursue its own selfish policies through corruption and exploitation. Would not the same pattern be required of that nation in order for it to find the way of faithfulness, and to find a genuine *solution* to its problems? Has the way to national righteousness changed significantly since the Lord spoke to Solomon? It would seem not. The only conceivable reason one might offer for refraining from bringing God's call for national repentance to modern nations would be that it is for some reason *futile* to do so today. But that would follow only if we were convinced that it is wrong to proclaim the solution to a problem when we cannot be guaranteed that our hearers will respond to that solution.

The difference between the political message to Israel and the message to modern nations is parallel to the difference between dealing with the problems of individual believers and individual unbelievers. If we counsel an unbeliever involved in an adulterous relationship, our advice about the ultimate solution to his problem is not different from the advice we would offer a believer in a similar situation. In each case the pattern to be followed is the parallel of the pattern of the solution for national disobedience: humility, prayer, repentance, forgiveness, and healing. Apart from this pattern there is no real solution to the underlying problems relating to adultery. There are not, from a Christian point of view, two different "solutions" to marital unfaithfulness, one for Christian adulterers and the other for non-Christian ones. The only difference between the two situations would be that the believer would be told to return to the way of faithfulness before God and the unbeliever would be invited to enter that way for the first time. Similarly, the proclaimed solution to Israel's political problems was a call to return to covenant faithfulness; but modern nations must be told that the only solution to the problems that plague their political lives is to enter into the way of obedience to the will of God.

Furthermore, there is a questionable premise in the argument that seeks to set aside the analogy between the prophets' relationship to Israel and the Christian's relationship to modern nations. The Old Testament prophets did not address their messages to Israel alone. A reading of Amos or Isaiah will reveal that they often stood in judgment of the political practices of other nations. For the calling of Israel into an obedient relationship with the Creator was meant to reveal to "the nations" the creative will of God for all mankind: "Turn to me and be saved, all the ends of the earth! For I am God, and there is no other" (Isaiah 45:22).

Without a doubt there are important questions as to how Christians are to go about proclaiming God's will to nations today. We shall return to these questions further on and content ourselves for the present with the general point that God has not ceased to be concerned with matters of national obedience and disobedience.

INCONSISTENCY AND SELECTIVITY

We have reviewed some of the major considerations that have consciously led to political inactivity on the part of many Christians. It should also be mentioned that Christians have been, at times, very selective—and even blatantly inconsistent—in their appeals to these considerations. They have denounced the sex habits of Hollywood while ignoring graft and corruption in the centers of political power. They have called for legislation to control Sunday business and the sale of alcohol but have refused to "meddle in politics" on voting rights and discriminatory employment practices. They have been concerned over the failure of science textbooks used in the public schools to emphasize man's creation in God's image, but they have too seldom spoken out against public laws and practices that oppress races of men who reflect that image. In the name of "separation of church and state" they have remained silent on matters of their nations' foreign policies, while freely criticizing the domestic policies of Communist countries. Under the guise of awaiting the transformation of all things they have enthusiastically supported the status quo. They have denounced the false prophets of political radicalism, while praying at the breakfasts of faithless kings and endorsing a spiritually destructive culture dispensed by greedy secular high priests.

Of course, inconsistency and selectivity are a mark of our sinful condition, and it is unlikely that any of our endeavors—including this present discussion—will completely avoid them. Sanctification is, after all, a process. But the demands of discipleship require us at least to struggle to become more obedient in the areas in which we have erred. Our hope is that the remainder of this study will begin to provide a framework for carrying on more effectively that struggle in the sphere of politics.

THE CHURCH: COMMUNITY AND POLITICS

"But you are a chosen race, a royal priesthood, a holy nation, God's own people, that you may declare the wonderful deeds of him who called you out of darkness into his marvelous light. Once you were no people but now you are God's people; once you had not received mercy but now you have received mercy."

I Peter 2:9-10

POLITICAL EVANGELISM, as we are using the term, is a task to which the church is called. A concern with political matters lies at the very center of the church's presence in the world. In order to make this perspective clear we must now discuss the nature of the church's calling, the purpose or purposes it has been created to fulfil as the community of God's people.

The term "church" can be understood in different senses, and we must begin with a rough account of what we have in mind in this context. We shall understand the church to be the New Testament version of the *people of God,* a community gathered in response to God's gracious work in Jesus Christ. The nature of this community can be understood in a narrow sense and in a broader one. First of all, the church has an "institutional" side. There are procedures to single out some members as preachers and teachers, others as supervisory officers, to set times for worship and education, to formulate and enforce rules for behavior, to plan and adopt budgets and the like. On the other hand, there is the broader scope of its existence—which includes the institutional aspect—for which some theologians have used the phrase "the church as organism." This broader sense also includes activities and relationships among Christians—members of the institutional church—that are more informal, less institutionalized: voluntary organizations and guilds, Bible study groups, prayer meetings, parties, family gatherings, fellowship among Christian friends, etc. We shall consider each area—the institutional and non-institutional—as important aspects of the life of the larger community of the people of God.

THE PRIMARY PURPOSE OF THE CHURCH: TWO VIEWS

What is the primary purpose for which the people of God have been gathered? Two very different answers have been given to this question, and each has its own implications for understanding the church's relation to the political sphere. First, there are those who insist that Christians are called by God to participate in the life of the church primarily for fellowship. The church is a gathering of Christians in retreat from the world; it is a community for edification and building up. On this view the community of believers has no corporate calling to be active in society. As one theologian has put it:

> No responsibility or service is imposed on the church *per se*. Service, like the gifts of the Spirit by whom service is wrought, is individual. It could not be otherwise. The common phrase, "the church's task," is, therefore, without Biblical foundation. It is only when individuals sense their personal responsibility and claim personal divine enablement that Christian work is done. On the other hand, there is no word written which by implication would hinder believers from being associated in a common cause which may be for convenience considered in the light of a combined result (Lewis Sperry Chafer, *Systematic Theology*, Volume IV, Dallas Seminary Press, 1948, p. 149).

If this understanding is correct, the church has no political task, simply because it has *no* task as such in the world. Tasks, activities of service in the world, are matters of individual calling. The church may—and probably should build individuals up for those tasks, and individuals may even find it convenient to work together in different areas with other Christians; but direct involvement in "service" activities is not the calling of the church as such.

A very different view of the primary purpose of the gathered people of God is reflected in recent emphases on "the church as mission." As one proponent of that view puts it:

> The church exists only *in actu*, in the execution of the apostolate, i.e., in the proclamation of the gospel of the Kingdom to the world. ... In no way can *mission* be viewed as *one* among other tasks to which the church is called. A church that knows that she is a function of the apostolate and that her very ground of existence lies in the proclamation of the Kingdom to the world, does not engage in missions, but she herself becomes mission, she becomes the living outreach of God to the world. That is why a church without mission is an absurdity. As soon as the church fails to become mission in the totality of her being, she thereby proves that she has been denaturalized into a temple or into some sort of association for the cultivation of one's personal religious life (J. C. Hoekendijk, *The Church Inside Out*, Westminster, 1964, pp. 43-44).

Here the church is seen as a people gathered for activity in the world; the church is not called to "retreat" but to be a focal point for confrontation with the world.

AN ALTERNATIVE VIEW: A TWOFOLD CALLING

Each of these views taken by itself is an inadequate understanding of the church and its primary purpose.

With the first view we must stress the importance of building fellowship in the community of God's people. Establishing community is central to the unfolding of the redemptive drama revealed in the Scriptures. This is obvious in the Old Testament, where we have the story of the election of a *nation,* a corporate body called by God to reveal in its communal life the glory of God to the nations.

But Christ's coming did not signal a radical shift in the mode of God's redemptive dealings with men. Some claim to see such a shift, from a primary concern with a corporate body in the Old Testament to a primary—if not exclusive—emphasis on the *individual's* relationship with God in the New Testament. But such a view fails to see that the New Testament succumbs no more than the Old to the sort of individualism that sees man in isolation from his fellow men. It is the *church* that calls men to turn from their evil ways; and it calls them into fellowship with God by inviting them to become engrafted into itself, the Body of Christ on earth, the Body God has chosen to be the community in which and through which he makes his glory known among men.

The church as the Body of Christ is a redeemed human community, in which those who have been rescued from the reign of sin may experience wholeness and reconciliation, a restoration of the dignity of human relationships.

Throughout the biblical record, then, God's redemptive dealings are with a people, a community established by his sovereign and electing grace, whose communal life together is, in itself, meant to be an instrument of his redemptive purposes in the world. Israel, by its very existence as a national community, was meant to be "a light to the nations," a *model* of collective obedience to the will of God. Similarly, the church—as the "new Israel"—is meant to be a paradigmatic community, whose life together demonstrates the triumphs of God's grace in human communal existence.

Building up the community of the people of God is not only central to the church's calling, but also especially important in the present age. On every level of human community today—in the community of nations, within the nation itself, in the city, on the university campus, even among the members of the family—one of the most pressing questions is, How can individuals and groups with diverse interests and concerns live together in even a minimal degree of cooperation and harmony? In an age troubled by that question it is crucial for God's people to realize their calling and demonstrate to the world that life together is indeed possible.

But the church may not be content to develop *merely* internally. Rather (and here we must echo the emphasis of the second view of the church's purpose) the church has an aggressive mission to perform in the world. That mission is this: the church must spread itself, it must call men everywhere to repent and to enter into participation in the community of the people of God. The church as God's "showpiece" community must share with the world the transformed life to which God, through the church, calls men. The church must invite the world to become what it is already in process of becoming, a community living in full obedience to God's revealed will for men.

THE CHURCH AS A POLITICAL COMMUNITY

Normally when the relationship between Christianity and politics is discussed, the focus is exclusively on the political structures of the larger human community in which the church participates. What is often overlooked is the fact that the church, in its own "internal" life, is itself a political community. As James Gustafson puts it:

> The political structure of the Church . . . is the *patterns of relationships and action through which policy is determined and social power exercised.* As a human society the Church must determine policy, and it must have the necessary social power to act in the light of its decisions. It defines its nature and task; it develops the means needed to achieve its mission in the world; it finds the necessary forms of social power to achieve some of its goals. Patterns exist through which authority is granted or assumed by particular persons in order to perform particular duties (*Treasure in Earthen Vessels,* Harper, 1961, p. 31).

Many would feel that talk about the "politics" of the Christian community is an admission of something less than noble. The political sphere is often thought of in terms of purely coercive or manipulative activity. This is clearly the sense in which Kate Millet uses the term in her book *Sexual Politics.* She introduces her subject by citing passages from the novelist Henry Miller, who describes sexual activities in the language of coercion, manipulation, and conquest. Then, offering the observation that "what the reader is experiencing at this juncture is a nearly supernatural sense of *power*—should the reader be a male," she concludes: "It is a case of sexual *politics* at the fundamental level of copulation" (p. 6; italics added). Thus she closely links together coercion, power, and politics.

The close connection between coercion and political power is in accordance with part of the biblical understanding of "power." The New Testament speaks often about a power present in the created order, a power that breeds corruption and operates through coercion and manipulation. Not only does this power bring imbalance and disintegration to individual lives and intimate human relationships, it also extends throughout the created order to bring all spheres of human activity, including the political, under its control.

But while the New Testament speaks often of power, it does not speak of power *as such*. Rather, it speaks of two *kinds* of power operating in the created order. One is the evil power of darkness, the power of Satan's rule. This power corrupts and distorts. The other is the power of God, which was dramatically infused into the present order through the mighty act by which God's Son was raised from the dead. This power delivers individuals from Satan's power and remakes them after the image of Jesus Christ. It frees them from the destructive and manipulative urges that consume all those who pretend to sit on the throne that belongs only to the Creator.

The life in which power is exercised as manipulation is accurately described by the social critic Paul Goodman. In such a life,

> to be prestigious and in a position to make decisions, is taken to be the social good itself, apart from any functions that it is thought to make possible. The pattern of dominance-and-submission has then been internalized and, by its clinch, fills up the whole of experience. If a man is not continually proving his potency, his mastery of others and of himself, he becomes prey to a panic of being defeated and victimized. Every vital function must therefore be used as a means of proving or it is felt as a symptom of weakness. Simply to enjoy, produce, learn, give or take, love or be angry (rather than cool), is to be vulnerable (*People or Personnel and Like a Conquered Province*, Vintage Books, 1968, p. 184).

In contrast to this pattern, with its echoes of the tempter's promise "You will be like God," becoming a beneficiary of God's liberating power means freedom to engage in a way of life that is much like the "peaceful functioning" Goodman goes on to promise: it is to be able to produce and learn without having to accumulate wealth and privileged position; it is to be free from the fear of appearing vulnerable and losing one's pretended mastery over men and things; it is to gain the freedom to serve, to be capable of simple and honest love and anger. All of this becomes possible when one no longer lives "the lie," but instead confesses one's sin and knows the acceptance and forgiveness of God's grace.

The contrast between God's power and the power of sin is made very clear in Romans 1. After celebrating the presence of "the power of God unto salvation," Paul delineates the scope and extent of the corrupting power of sin. To be outside the sphere of God's saving power is to be given over to a process that can only end in complete disintegration and death. Paul's choice of mainly sexual examples in verses 24-28 should not blind us to the pervasiveness of the corrupting power he is describing, for there is a kind of promiscuity that can characterize the social, business, and political areas as well. To take delight in the failures and losses of others is also to be given over to "dishonorable passions." To seek to manipulate others and to bend their wills to one's own selfish goals is also to engage in "shameless acts." To use one's God-given rational faculties to plot self-enhancement is also to reflect the workings of a "base mind."

The corrupting power of sin does not only manifest itself in one-to-one relationships. It also comes to be reflected in the patterns and procedures that govern our social, economic, and political lives. C. Freeman Sleeper, in a perceptive study of the black power

44

concept in the light of the biblical conception of power (*Black Power and Christian Responsibility*, Abingdon, 1969, especially Chapter 8), suggests that distorted forms of power are characterized by the presence of distrust, domination, alienation and either a false optimism or a premature despair. On the other hand, he suggests, the responsible patterns of power to which the Scriptures call us are characterized by faithfulness, which involves mutual accountability and responsibility; freedom, not *from* institutional structures but *for* the shaping and preserving of structures that promote mutual integrity; love, which is manifested in sacrificial service, sharing, and mutual support; and hope, which realistically assesses the potential for future growth together.

While the political sphere has to do with power, then, we must not limit our understanding of political power to its coercive and manipulative aspects. This is an important point in our discussion. It is not only Kate Millet and Marxist political theorists who limit politics to this. Conservative Christians can also be heard to speak as if the political realm *as such* is a "necessary evil" brought about by God because of man's fallen condition. But if we regard the political aspect of human life as having to do with those patterns of authority, accountability, collective decision-making, and corporate responsibility necessary in some form for community life, coercive and manipulative patterns will be seen as the sinful or fallen conditions of political life, as opposed to those patterns possible under unfallen or regenerate human conditions.

Perhaps an example will clarify this. Imagine a totally "sanctified" human community, of which all the members are freed from sinful impulses. Imagine further that the corporate worship of God is still one

45

important part of the life of that community. If it is desirable that there is a time when the entire community gathers for worship, some *regulation* toward that end will have to be operative in the community. For, if there is in such a community a time to worship and a time to play, a time to dance and a time to work, it is not at all clear that every sinless individual in that community will choose automatically to worship or play or dance or work at the same time. This is not because of any sinful influence, but simply because each individual would presumably retain some uniqueness of temperament and inclination. Hence, regulations might well operate in such a community. Furthermore, the entire group might share in the decision-making processes that produced such regulations. Thus, such a community would have some sort of *political* structuring, albeit not one characterized by coercion and manipulation.

The political structures of the church are easiest to recognize in its life as an institution. But there is a sense in which even informal, noninstitutionalized collective relationships have a "political" aspect to them. The title of Wilfred Sheed's novel *Office Politics* uses the term in a somewhat extended but not completely inappropriate sense. To the extent that certain patterns of decision-making, accountability, and authority-distribution—however informal or uncodified—emerge wherever two or three or more are gathered together for some roughly defined purpose, it is not entirely out of place to speak, without disparaging it, of the "politics" of the family unit, the classroom, or the Bible study group.

The church, we have seen, must deal with political relationships in two general areas. It must think of its own political structures and relationships, which pattern the institutional and noninstitutional life of the people of God, and it must heed its participation in and relation to the political structures of the larger human community. In fact, its concern with its own political patterns is, in an important sense, more central than its concern with those of the larger community. This is not said to denigrate the church's witness to and in that community, but to stress the importance of the church's building up its own community as a necessary preparation for its larger witness. For part of the calling of the people of God is to demonstrate in their life together that it is possible for men to live, cooperate, and make decisions with one another in an atmosphere of trust, openness, mutual service, and hope. The strength of the church's political witness to the larger nation, and to the community of nations, must lie in the fact that it can point to its own life together as a model of communal harmony based on collective obedience to the will of God. And it can testify that the political patterns of its own community reflect and point to the total transformation of all things that is the hope of the promised Kingdom.

"A HOLY NATION"

The foregoing makes clear that the Apostle was not being swept away by his poetic instincts when he addressed the New Testament church as a holy nation (I Peter 2:9). Several points must be noted in relation to the appropriateness of this image.

First, the image brings out the important continuity between the Israel of the old covenant and the church of the new covenant. In each case God has gathered a people in whose community life he restores the com-

47

munion between himself and man, and between man and man, which was lost through the fall into sin. A purely individualistic understanding of the Christian life, then, is a serious distortion of New Testament Christianity.

Second, the image of the church as holy nation helps correct the tendency to anti-institutionalism that often characterizes the attitudes of Christians. The Christian, as a member of the church, must not oppose institutions as such. Rather, he is called to participate in the redemption and transformation of institutional life.

Third, an awareness of the legitimate, even necessary, role of political processes in the community of God's people should make us more sensitive to the need for the continual, responsible re-formation of "church government" and to the defects—which because of the presence of redemptive power in the world *need* not exist—of the political processes of the larger human community.

Fourth, the idea of Christians existing together as a "nation" within the larger nation in which they find themselves can be a helpful reminder of the unique life-style to which Christians are called. Other groups have advanced the "nation-within-a-nation" concept to symbolize their commitment to values and styles of living that differ from those of their fellow citizens. The "Woodstock nation" theme of the counter culture is an example of this. Another case is found in this description of the mood of a contemporary people:

> Movement, independence—these are the watchwords of the Navajos today. They speak of their tribe more often as the "nation"—and rightly so, since Navajo nationhood exists by treaty, signed with the United States in 1868. The tribe has its own legislature, police and courts. Except for traffic regulations, state laws do not apply to Indians in the reservation. The Federal government retains juris-

diction only over the so-called 14 major crimes, such as murder, rape, and robbery.

But the Navajos want to be more a part of the United States as well. During the past decade, two Navajos have served in the New Mexico Legislature (Ralph Looney, "The Navajo Nation Looks Ahead," *National Geographic*, December 1972, p. 747).

Of course, there are dissimilarities between the sense in which the Christian community should think of itself as a nation and this illustration. But the example is helpful because the church, too, might be thought of as having "its own legislature, police and courts." And the sense of tentativeness in the Navajo's commitment to the American nation, coupled with his genuine desire to participate in that nation, is instructive for the church.

Fifth, the recognition of a distinct "national identity" among members of the Body of Christ can keep before us our ties with Christians who live under different secular governments, with whom we have bonds that transcend and override our commitments to governments and groups outside the church.

Finally, the Apostle's nation-image can aid in keeping before our minds the fact that, no matter what "earthly" allegiances we have to political powers, we are members of another society that places significant obligations on us, namely, the theocratic community over which Jesus Christ is King. When an earlier generation of Christians sang, "I walk with the King! Hallelujah!" they were often so enthusiastic about the personal joys involved in that walk that they de-emphasized the fact that their personal communion was indeed with a *King*. If we fail to remedy such a lack of sensitivity to the political lordship of Christ, we are risking serious departure from the way of obedient discipleship.

CHURCH
AND STATE

"The world has hated them because they are not of the world, even as I am not of the world. I do not pray that thou shouldst take them out of the world, but that thou shouldst keep them from the evil one. They are not of the world, even as I am not of the world. Sanctify them in the truth; thy word is truth. As thou didst send me into the world, so I have sent them into the world."

John 17:14-18

WE HAVE DISCUSSED the appropriateness of thinking of the church as a "holy nation." But whatever the relevant similarities between ancient Israel and the contemporary community of the people of God, at least one important difference comes immediately to mind. The church, as an institution alongside other human institutions, exists under the rule of "secular" human governments. Israel with its internal government stood, in responsibility, directly before God. The church, however, with its internal government is also responsible to other human governments. We must now ask: What must be the general posture of the church in relation to the government under whose rule it functions, whether that be the government of the United States, or of Great Britain, or of the Soviet Union?

ROMANS 13:1-7

It would be difficult, in any discussion of the church's relationship to secular government, to ignore completely Paul's remarks in Romans 13. We shall not discuss this passage at great length. (Readers interested in an extended discussion will do well to read Chapter 10 of John Howard Yoder's *The Politics of Jesus,*

Eerdmans, 1972.) Two comments will suffice us here.

First, if we understand Paul's remarks in the light of the entire biblical message, we should see clearly that Romans 13 does not justify us in making an unconditional commitment to any earthly government. Arthur Gish's comments along these lines are both helpful and misleading:

> Even in Romans 13:1, the most conservative view of the state in the New Testament, it is affirmed that the state exists only by the consent of God and is thus under God. Any authority that claims ultimacy for itself takes on totalitarian and demonic qualities. For this reason the Roman Empire is described in Revelation 13 as the beast which will kill all who refuse to worship it. This is an apt description of a totalitarian state. The Lordship of God means that no finite group can claim ultimacy for itself, for only God is Lord. Thus the Christian cannot pledge allegiance to any institution. The Christian, because of his higher allegiance, is by nature disloyal to all institutions (*The New Left and Christian Radicalism*, Eerdmans, 1970, p. 87).

Gish is correct to point out that the entire biblical context requires us to balance Paul's advice here against the real possibility that a government may become a "beast," obedience to whom is not worthy of those whose names are written "in the book of life of the Lamb that was slain" (Revelation 13:8).

But for the Christian to consider his allegiance to a particular government as conditional does not amount to disloyalty to human governments as such. By analogy, it is possible to be committed to ardently supporting and promoting respect for the institution of marriage without maintaining that each married person has an *unconditional* obligation to keep his marriage intact. Most Christians allow for biblically legitimate divorce on the ground of adultery. This does not mean that they are disloyal to the institution of marriage. At the very least Paul seems to be saying here that it is better for men to live under government than not to and that Christians ought to promote respect for government. Gish's apparent anti-institutionalism might lead one to conclude simply that no government at all is preferable to a bad government. But there is another option that seems to be more compatible with Paul's intent: a *good* government is preferable to either a bad government or no government at all.

Our second comment on this passage is that contemporary appeals to Romans 13 often fail to realize the implications of Paul's teaching for contemporary *democratic* societies. On the most conservative reading of this passage, as applied to Paul's audience, the Apostle was insisting that the authority and mandate to govern, even in totalitarian societies, are given to human beings by God, so that one may not lightly dismiss the obligation to respect and obey political powers. But in modern democracies the power of national leaders is derived from the populace, which is the *primary* locus of God-given authority. Built into the very process is the possibility of review, debate, re-examination, election, and defeat. Given such a framework, for Christians simply to acquiesce in a present policy is to *fail to respect* the governing authorities—in the primary sense, as understood in democratic theory. Democratic government grants Christians the right publicly to criticize, review, debate, and challenge current procedures and policies. Under those conditions, the message of Romans 13 imposes on them the duty to make use of that right.

I PETER 2:9-17

We talked in the last chapter about Peter's address to the New Testament church as a "holy nation."

Since he relates this address to the church's life in a secular nation, we must now look more closely at the context of his address:

> But you are a chosen race, a royal priesthood, a holy nation, God's own people, that you may declare the wonderful deeds of him who called you out of darkness into his marvellous light. Once you were no people but now you are God's people; once you had not received mercy but now you have received mercy (I Peter 2:9-10).

Each of these images links the church to Old Testament Israel. The dominant image is the calling and forming of a people to take over Israel's role as a "light" to the nations of the earth. The status of Christians as a people derives solely from the electing mercy of God and is linked to the purposes of that election.

Peter goes on to describe the general posture of this elected people toward their fellow men (verses 11-12):

> Beloved, I beseech you as aliens and exiles to abstain from the passions of the flesh that wage war against your soul. Maintain good conduct among the Gentiles, so that in case they may speak against you as wrongdoers, they may see your good deeds and glorify God on the day of visitation.

Two closely parallel tensions are referred to here. First, the allegiance of God's people to the civil society in which they find themselves must be like that of "aliens and exiles." In other words, their commitment is conditional and tentative. But this must not deter them from maintaining "good conduct among the Gentiles." Their good deeds play an important part in their calling. Second, with regard to the nature of the "good deeds," there is a tension between what will be presently counted as good deeds by the Gentiles and what they will recognize as such "on the day of visitation." Clearly Christians are called to do works that are pleasing and obedient to God. Yet, they must make an effort to portray their faithful lives in the best possible light to "the Gentiles." When those efforts are met with hostility and slander, of course, they must take comfort in the hope of future vindication.

"The day of visitation" is a somewhat ambiguous reference. Commentators disagree whether it refers to a future time of accounting before God or to the culmination of a civil investigation of rumors that there was misconduct on the part of Christians. In either case, the thrust of Peter's advice seems to require Christians to act justly within the bonds of civil society as well as to remember their accountability to God as his chosen people.

The appropriate attitude of Christians toward civil authority is further specified in the next five verses:

> Be subject for the Lord's sake to every human institution, whether it be to the emperor as supreme, or to governors as sent by him to punish those who do wrong and to praise those who do right. For it is God's will that by doing right you should put to silence the ignorance of foolish men. Live as free men, yet without using your freedom as a pretext for evil; but live as servants of God. Honor all men. Love the brotherhood. Fear God. Honor the emperor.

Here the need for recognizing the positive role of human institutions is stressed, and the need for blamelessness before civil authorities and fellow citizens is repeated. But the Christian commitment to the maintenance of law and order cannot be blind and mechanical: it is, rather, freely and responsibly offered. There is only one perspective that can rescue us from both unthinking subservience, in which our freedom before God is sacrificed, and a false spirit of civil rebellion, in which we fail to promote orderliness and justice. In the Apostle's words: *"Live as servants of God."*

This life of service is spelled out in terms of our attitudes toward four persons or groups who make claims upon us: "Honor all men. Love the brotherhood. Fear God. Honor the emperor." These four attitudes summarize the Christian's obligations to two distinct groups—civil society with its appointed leaders and the Christian community under the rule of God. The same verb, "honor" (Greek, *timao*), is used in relation to "all men" and "the emperor." This verb is sometimes used in the New Testament in relation to our attitudes toward God the Father and Jesus Christ (it is used for both in John 5:23), but it is also used to designate the proper attitude toward parents (Matthew 15:4; 19:19) and widows (I Timothy 5:3). When applied to human beings, "honor" seems to connote at least a formal respect and concern for the well-being of those to whom it is offered. On the other hand, the verbs used to describe the requirements toward the brotherhood and God—"love" (*agapao*) and "fear" (*phobeo*), respectively—designate attitudes of genuine delight in the well-being of fellow Christians, and a deep sense of awe and reverence before God.

The upshot of Peter's message seems to be this: the people of God are called to have a unique identity among the nations of the earth. They constitute a community whose primary loyalty is to God as revealed in Jesus Christ. But they must seek to work out this loyalty as much as possible within the framework of peaceful relations with civil society. Just as Jesus Christ was sent into the world "not to condemn the world, but that the world might be saved through him" (John 3:17), so his Body must assume a stance toward civil society that is not one of contempt or condemnation, but one of willingness to adopt a servant-role among men, so that God may be glorified through their good works. This role must always be pursued, however, in full knowledge of an ultimate commitment to the lordship of Christ, who, though he came not to condemn but to save, came to the point where he had to suffer at the hands of human authority. The Christian's freedom is such that it too may lead to the cross.

In short, the pattern to which the people of God must seek to conform in their relationships to the larger human community is that for which Christ prayed on their behalf: "I do not pray that thou shouldst take them out of the world, but that thou shouldst keep them from the evil one" (John 17:15).

5

PATTERNS FOR CHRISTIAN COMMUNITY

"Beloved, I beseech you as aliens and exiles to abstain from the passions of the flesh that wage war against your soul. Maintain good conduct among the Gentiles so that in case they speak against you as wrongdoers, they may see your good deeds and glorify God on the day of visitation."

I Peter 2:11-12

THE COMMUNITY OF THE PEOPLE OF GOD is called to become a model community in the world as a witness to the triumphs of God's grace. How ought such a community to be structured? In what respects will it differ significantly from other human communities? We have already suggested some answers to these questions, but it will be helpful to pursue these matters in some more detail. We cannot hope to develop here a full-blown Christian political theory. However, we can note in passing how some of the key concepts of political theory might be viewed from a biblical perspective.

THE SOCIAL BOND

Implicit in any view of the norms that should govern community life is an answer to the question: Why ought men to live together at all? Traditionally, there have been two very different responses. One, sometimes called individualism, views each man as complete and autonomous apart from the social bond. If such basically independent and asocial individuals are to enter into social relationships, there must be some legitimate incentive for taking that step. Although the various individualistic theories differ about the precise content of that justification, they generally view the social bond as justified in terms of the self-interest of each individual involved. Community-formation or the social contract is a means for each individual to gain for himself certain goods which are more accessible through social living than they would be in a nonsocial state. In short, the social bond is justified in terms of the convenience it affords for each participating individual, although that convenience may be spelled out with respect to somewhat vague, "long-range" goals.

A very different answer to this basic question is found in a view that is sometimes labeled organicism. Organicist theories view men as, in some sense, "organically" related. The individual is significantly incomplete apart from the social bond. "No man is an island." In response to our question, Why should people live together? an organicist might answer: Because apart from the social bond we are not *men*!

These two basic social theories have analogues in doctrines concerning the nature of the church. Individualistic Christians often place great stress on the individual Christian's relationship to God as prior to, and distinct from, his relationship to other Christians. The question, then, of why the individual Christian ought to unite together with other Christians is sometimes answered in very pragmatic terms. A common answer is that there are "blessings" that the individual can receive from fellowship with "those of like precious faith," blessings to which he might not have access otherwise.

On the other side are those views of the church that emphasize the "organism" or "body" metaphors of the New Testament. Here the call to faith in God is understood as a call to participation in the visible church. Understood in this way, the dictum, "Outside of the church there is no salvation," would be a straight-forward version of this view.

Each of these areas social theory and ecclesi ology—is important for the Christian view of community. The question about the nature of the basic social bond has to do with the purposes for which man was created; the question about the ecclesiastical bond has to do with the purposes for which man has been redeemed in Christ. In the first area, individualism would seem to be seriously defective, since man was created for fellowship with God, as well as for fellowship with his own kind in obedience before God. Organicism rightly stresses this interrelationship on the human level; but a heavy reliance on the metaphors of the body can be misleading. It is not enough to assert simply the "organic" unity of mankind, for sin has made it possible for men to remain in rebellion against one another in a way that bodily parts could not sustain alienation and yet remain alive. In the final analysis, the relationship between one human being and another is not simply like the relationship between, say, a heart and a liver.

Gordon Clark has rightly pointed out in relation to political theory that "all the nontheistic systems assume that the present condition of man is normal; the Christian system views actual humanity as abnormal" (*A Christian View of Men and Things,* Eerdmans, 1952, p. 138). Thus, a Christian view concerning the norms for community life must go beyond a discussion of the nature of the basic social bond to attend to the redemptive remedy for the sin which has distorted man's created sociality. How, then, must we view the nature of the Christian social bond? Here, too, individualism has its serious defects. The creation of a "people" is not a mere convenience in God's redemptive economy; it is central to his redemptive dealings with men. God does not merely call isolated individuals into fellowship with himself; he works graciously to complete his creative purposes for man, by restoring the full community that was disrupted by sin's entrance into human affairs.

But organicism also has dangerous implications for a view of Christian community. For God created *individual* men, each of whom has a unique status and responsibility before him; and his redemptive activity as well deals with individuals in their uniqueness. Any view of the church that would absorb the individual into the whole or reduce individuals to institutional roles seriously fails to account for this uniqueness.

GOVERNMENT AND AUTHORITY

Any theory concerning the norms for human community, we said, is based on a theory about the nature of the social bond. This can be seen clearly in relation to the question, Which form of government is best? We cannot judge this or that form of government as "best" unless we have some purpose or goal for government in view. In order to decide how a community can be best governed we must have some idea as to why it exists.

In both secular and ecclesiastical tradition, individualistic theories have often leaned toward democratic forms of government and organicistic theories toward authoritarianism. When the social bond is justified, as it is in individualism, in terms of the private good of each individual, a form of government that guarantees the maximum freedom possible in a social context for each individual best fulfils the purposes of the social contract. On the other hand, if individuals are seen as organically interrelated, a form of government that maximizes the harmony of the parts may be seen as more desirable.

Most popular conceptions of democracy are based on individualistic theories. As such they are inapplicable to Christian community. Ultimately to justify democratic decision-making processes by the value of making one's *own* decisions (or "doing your own thing") and finding one's *own* happiness is inadequate for discussing government in a Christian community.

Against the influence of popular democratic theory the Christian must insist that Christian community exists in order to do the will of God and to show forth his glory. The church of Jesus Christ is a community conscious of its origins not in the designs and hopes of men but in the electing mercies of God. The "best" form of government, then, is that which enables the community most adequately to serve the Lord who is the head of the church.

These words will sound strange in the contemporary milieu with its prevalent stress on the dogma of human autonomy to the degree that any form of submission to higher authority is seen as at least regrettable and often as a positive evil. In the face of criticisms from this perspective the response must be made that the Christian's obedience to the authoritative will of God is in no way an authoritarianism of the despotic variety. Christian community exists for the purpose of doing the will of God, but the will of God is directed toward the good of the community. God calls men to obedience, not as some dictator who imposes his foreign desires on his fellow men, but as the Creator who shaped man out of love and who redeems man for the purpose of restoring the dignity and richness of human relationships.

Of crucial importance is that the God of the Scriptures calls men freely to serve him. This theme so pervades the biblical message that even the most rigidly "predestinarian" views of salvation have struggled to acknowledge it. A good example is found in the Canons of the Synod of Dort (1618-1619):

> This grace of regeneration does not treat men as senseless stocks and blocks, nor take away their will and its properties, neither does violence thereto; but spiritually quickens, heals, corrects, and at the same time sweetly and powerfully bends it, that where carnal rebellion and resistance formerly prevailed a ready and sincere spiritual obedience begins to reign; in which the true and spiritual restoration and freedom of our will consist.

The premium that the Scriptures place on free response and noncoercion must be reflected in the decision procedures of the community of the people of God. Under sinful conditions this may be an ideal that can only be approximated. The censure of someone who consistently violates the norms of Christian community may be a necessary form of "coercion." Nevertheless, Christian community must be characterized by the promotion of continuing dialogue, "the benefit of the doubt," patience, frankness, and charity. All of these should be built into both the form and the mood of decision-making.

Two further points must be made concerning the authority patterns of Christian community. First, the passages in the New Testament that use the body metaphor make it clear that the tasks of Christian community must be distributed in accordance with the various gifts God bestows on individual members.

> For as in one body we have many members, and all the members do not have the same function, so we, though many, are one body in Christ, and individually members one of another. Having gifts that differ according to the

> grace given to us, let us use them: if prophecy, in pro-
> portion to our faith; if service, in our serving; he who
> teaches, in his teaching; he who exhorts, in his exhorta-
> tion; he who contributes, in liberality; he who gives aid,
> with zeal; he who does acts of mercy, with cheerfulness
> (Romans 12:4-8).

Paul makes it clear that these gifts are to be taken into account in communal decision-making. This emphasis excludes a "mob-democracy" kind of rule.

But at the same time decision-making by this membership with its diverse gifts must not be shaped by an authoritarian spirit. Paul begins Romans 12 with the insistence that only a transformation that releases us from conformity to the world can prepare us to "prove what is the will of God" (vs. 2). And in the rest of the chapter he warns against pride (vs. 3), haughtiness and conceit (vs. 16), and vengeance (vs. 19). Elsewhere, too, Paul makes it clear that the Christian must operate with a concept of authority that radically differs from that of the world. In Ephesians 5, after insisting that wives must "be subject" to their husbands (vs. 24), he goes on to admonish husbands to "love your wives, as Christ loved the church and gave himself up for her" (vs. 25), which is to say that a husband must "love his wife as himself" (vs. 33). In the Christian community, authority cannot be separated from service and self-sacrifice.

THE SPIRIT OF BELONGING

The spirit that must permeate Christian community is captured in a few words by the Heidelberg Catechism, in the opening words of its answer to the question: "What is your only comfort in life and in death?": "That I, with body and soul, both in life and in death, am not my own, but belong to my faithful

69

Savior Jesus Christ. . . ." To be able to take comfort in the fact that "I am not my own" is an attitude that radically distinguishes the Christian way from the individualistic spirit—whose chief comfort seems to lie in the assurance that "I'm my own person" or "I did it *my* way."

The Christian's primary personal, social, and political security is rooted in the love of a Savior from whom no principalities can separate him. But to belong to Jesus Christ is to belong to all of that to which Christ has given himself. It is to belong in a special and intimate way to all others for whom Christ died—namely, the company of the redeemed. To find one's comfort in belonging to Jesus Christ is also to consider it a comfort to belong to his people.

The point is put well by Dietrich Bonhoeffer:

> Without Christ there is discord between God and man and between man and man. Christ became the Mediator and made peace with God and among men. Without Christ we should not know God, we could not call upon Him, nor come to Him. But without Christ we also would not know our brother, nor could we come to him. The way is blocked by our own ego. Christ opened up the way to God and to our brother. Now Christians can live with one another in peace; they can love and serve one another; they can become one. But they can continue to do so only by way of Jesus Christ. Only in Jesus Christ are we one, only through him are we bound together. To eternity he remains the one Mediator.
>
> . . . God Himself has undertaken to teach brotherly love; all that men can add to this is to remember this divine instruction and the admonition to excel in it more and more. When God was merciful, when He revealed Jesus Christ to us as our Brother, when He won our hearts by His love, this was the beginning of our instruction in divine love. When God was merciful to us, we learned to be merciful with our brethren. When we received forgiveness instead of judgment, we, too, were made ready to forgive our brethren. What God did to us, we then owed to others. The more we received, the more we were able

to give; and the more meager our brotherly love, the less were we living by God's mercy and love. Thus God Himself taught us to meet one another as God has met us in Christ (*Life Together*, SCM Press, 1954, pp. 13-15).

Belonging to Christ also means belonging to the redemptive work that he made his own in his life on earth. It is to give oneself completely to the work of mercy by which Christ reached out to the spiritually broken, the poor, the sick, and the oppressed. In this sense, the Christian way is rooted in very different values, commitments, and comforts from the motivations found among those whose loyalties are to this present age. And so the path of Christian discipleship and the life of the people of God constitute a radical alternative to contemporary styles of living.

There can be no doubt that a community that reflected this spirit in all aspects of its life would find its own political structures and processes in a state of continual transformation. Our discussion here of the kind of interrelationships that would be experienced in such a community has, of course, an idealistic tone to it. Further on we must deal explicitly with the issues of "idealism" and "realism." For the present we must stress that while the people of God must be able to point to their own life together as a political model in their witness to the world, the present life of the people of God is not one of accomplished and complete reconciliation but one of a process toward that goal. With that in mind, it is clear that while the church must be a model to the world, the Christian community itself is in need of a model to guide it in the process of growing into the communal obedience to which it is called. The transformed notions of sociality, government, authority, and selfhood outlined in this chapter are important elements of that model.

6

STRATEGIES FOR
POLITICAL EVANGELISM

"Speaking the truth in love, we are to grow up in every way into him who is the head, into Christ, from whom the whole body, joined and knit together by every joint with which it is supplied, when each part is working properly, makes bodily growth and upbuilds itself in love."

Ephesians 4:15-16

IN THE PREVIOUS THREE CHAPTERS we have paid considerable attention to various aspects of the communal life of the people of God. This has not been meant merely as an aside. Our main concern is still political evangelism. But the Christian's political witness to the unbelieving world cannot be separated from the context or base out of which he speaks and acts. Political evangelism must be an outgrowth of our life together as the people of God. With this in mind we can understand how even the most separatist of Christian groups, insofar as they have ascertained the need for a distinctive Christian community, have not been completely off the mark. What they have failed to recognize is the need for viewing their communal life as a base of operation for an active Christian witness in the world.

Political evangelism involves two intimately related aspects. The first is building and sustaining Christian community. We shall now discuss the strategies that may be employed in relation to the second aspect—the evangelistic outreach of that community.

STRATEGIES AND GOALS

For a statement of the overall goal of evangelistic activity we can turn again to I Peter 2: "that you may declare the wonderful deeds of him who has called you out of darkness into his marvelous light" (vs. 9). Evangelism is concerned to show forth the full glories of the Kingdom of God among men, with an eye to the day when that Kingdom will reign over the entire earth. The supreme test of the worthiness of our strategies in evangelism is whether they are compatible with this goal.

By stressing the need for the compatibility of our strategies with our overall goal, we can avoid the error of thinking that our strategy must consist simply in the announcement of our goal. The popular cartoon caricature of a bearded, white-robed figure carrying a sign proclaiming "The End is Near" is a good example of the narrow identification of strategy with goal.

This narrow identification has often been made in what is popularly known as "personal evangelism." Evangelism ought never to be identified simply with the verbal articulation of the biblical message. On the personal level it may demand that we question rather than proclaim; it may require nonverbal demonstrations of concern and compassion; it might even necessitate a struggle on our part to overcome the temptation to speak too readily. Generally speaking, a desire to bring the claims of Christ to another person should not be divorced from a genuine willingness to come to know the unique needs of that individual. The proclamation of the gospel is not an end in itself. It is directed toward people, in all of their relationships. Thus, it is not enough that we proclaim the good news clearly, as if our task were simply to "get the message out." Our task is to get the message to persons. A straightforward proclamation of the message can often be a very ineffective means toward that end if we do not pay attention to the interpersonal context in which that proclamation is made.

There is an important educational dimension to the task of evangelism; we must also teach men what deciding to confess Jesus as Lord is all about. As good teachers, we must look for patience, discernment, and a willingness to labor with those whom we must teach. It is not enough, then, to be satisfied that we gave someone a clear-cut choice as to whom he will serve. We must also strive to create the best conditions for the effective communication of the Christian message. We cannot say all of this, of course, without also acknowledging that God can miraculously melt hardened hearts in an instant, and he can also use a Balaam's ass to articulate an effective witness. But we must not commit the error of confusing the possible with the desirable.

INTEGRATING THE ASPECTS OF EVANGELISM

Evangelism is a task of the people of God. Each member of the Christian community is responsible for the overall task of evangelism. No member of the Body of Christ can be exempt from this responsibility, precisely because each is a *member* of the Body and each exists for the sake of all that the Body is and does.

However, the degree to which an individual Christian personally participates in a particular evangelistic endeavor will depend on his gifts and the specific callings that correspond to these gifts. As Paul puts it in Ephesians 4:7-12:

> Grace was given to each of us according to the measure of Christ's gift. . . . And his gifts were that some should be apostles, some prophets, some evangelists, some pastors

77

and teachers, for the equipment of the saints, for the work of ministry, for building up the body of Christ. . . .

This clearly implies that some Christians will have as their major responsibility the maintenance of the internal health of the Body, preparing others for mission in the world, while others will be directly involved in that mission. Recognizing that the mission itself has many facets, we ought to be very wary of any claim that begins with the words: "The most important task that any Christian can be engaged in is . . . " and then proceeds to single out some *specific* task associated with the life or mission of the church.

To such endeavors as "personal" evangelism and political evangelism, no Christian can be completely removed from some direct relationship. Each of us is capable of communicating and regularly comes into contact with non-Christians; and all adult Christians have responsibilities as citizens, which force them to deal with their Christian duty in this area. But there are also special "gifts" in these matters and we should not expect that all Christians will be directly involved in them to the same degree and in the same manner.

How then are the various aspects of evangelistic activity to be integrated and coordinated? The simple answer is: by the grace of God. But, having acknowledged that, we must ask how we may be instruments of that grace. Of utmost importance is that each aspect of the evangelistic task of the church be engaged in with a sense of the *overall* work of evangelism. This means, simply, that Christians must not undercut the work of other Christians. Those whose work it is to call for a very personal response to Jesus Christ must not do so in a way that would denigrate the need for political witness. They must not give the impression

that submission to the lordship of Christ has no implications for a person's political life. This is not to say
that they must spell out those implications; it is unlikely that a person will be prepared to follow Christ in
the political sphere until he has experienced and reflected on the healing power of God in very personal
relationships. Sanctification, we say again, is a *process.*
It involves growth, even in the capacity to understand
the implications of the gospel.

Those who engage in a special way in political witness must also do so with a consciousness of the overall
evangelistic task. They must prayerfully support those
Christians who present the claims of Christ to individuals, and those who attempt to bring healing to
broken family relationships, and those who build up
the Body of Christ through the preaching and teaching
of the word. In all of these aspects of the life and
mission of the church, the spirit prescribed by Paul
ought to prevail: "I bid every one among you not to
think of himself more highly than he ought to think,
but to think with sober judgment, each according to
the measure of faith which God has assigned him"
(Romans 12:3).

Many of the difficulties involved in integrating various evangelistic activities would be diminished by a
stronger sense of Christian community and the felt
obligation of mutual accountability that would ac-
company such an awareness. Some ways of fostering
this will be proposed later in this chapter.

PREACHING AND POLITICAL EVANGELISM

We turn now to a much-discussed issue: what should
be the role of the institutional church in matters of
public policy? (Here, of course, we are thinking of the

political policies of the larger human community.) To what extent should the institutional church issue official or quasi-official pronouncements on military, economic, legislative, and judicial questions? This question has to do largely with the degree to which pastoral guidance should be given on these matters to members of the Christian community, for usually, even when official church proclamations have been directed to the general public and to government officials, their influence has been felt primarily within the Christian community. While much of what will be said here will apply to the declarations of synods, assemblies, bishops, denominational leaders, and study committees, we shall confine our discussion to the place of political pronouncements in "the preaching of the word."

The preacher of the word has been selected by the Christian community to provide guidance from God's word for the life of God's people. As such, his words have an official, or quasi-official, status. Should he, in the course of preaching, take a stand on a specific matter of public policy? If so, should he do this regularly or only under unusual circumstances?

Some are quick to reply that it is not within the sphere of the competence of the preacher to pronounce on social and political specifics. It is not easy to see the point of this claim. If the preacher is called to prepare the people of God for obedience to the lordship of Christ, steps should be taken to insure that he is generally competent to do so. Certainly some measures would be initiated if a preacher were discovered to be incompetent as an expositor of the Scriptures. Furthermore, it just does not seem to be necessarily true that all preachers are incompetent to make specific judgments in this area. Someone who turned to a preaching ministry after some years of teaching political science, for example, or in public office, or in the military, might well speak as an expert on such matters.

The real issue is not one of competence but of authority. Does the preacher of the word have the authority to speak on matters of political policy? One condition to be met is that the issue in question be one on which he can speak with the assurance that he is presenting, not merely his own words and concerns, but the words and concerns of the God of the Scriptures. This may occur in one of two ways. First, an issue might be of a sort for which a preacher can sense very clear guidance in the light of the Scriptures. Suppose a piece of legislation were offered which tended to promote a widespread deterioration of family bonds and had no obvious merits. In this case it would be quite clear that the Scriptures would require us to oppose, and not to support such a measure. Much the same would be true of a situation in which a government was pursuing, out of vengeance or confusion, a course of genocide against a certain class of innocent persons.

Second, an issue may be such that it is not clear to the preacher what specific stand ought to be taken, but where he senses that the considerations in the light of which the decision should be made are generally being ignored by the Christian community. Appropriate pastoral guidance in such a case might sound like this: "No matter how you decide, do *not* do so purely on the basis of your own financial security, etc."

In the former situation the preacher prescribes a specific decision or stand; in the latter he guides the people in their own personal decision-making and struggle by calling their attention to the relevant biblical principles and guidelines. Each of these approaches is in principle justifiable for the preacher to take. In deciding which to choose in relation to a given issue, a foremost concern must be that the approach is the best means, on that occasion, for building up the people of God for obedience in the political sphere. Here it is important to keep in mind that the pastoral and preaching ministry has an important educational task connected with it. In political, as with personal evangelism, a teacher cannot be concerned merely to "get the truth out." He must also be concerned effectively to communicate the truth to those whom he must teach.

While there is, then, no reason in principle why the preacher cannot prescribe specific political choices, doing so may not always—or even often—be the best way of promoting the political growth of the people of God. As a general rule, perhaps, he should try to enunciate the principles and guidelines that will aid them in their own decision-making, thus leaving room for the individual to engage in the process of struggle and maturation. This does not relieve him of responsibility for the political growth of his people; rather, he must see this as a means for promoting that growth. Also, we are suggesting this approach only as a tentative, general rule. There will be times (Nazi Germany affords a clear example) when there must be a clear proclamation and warning to the people of God concerning a political situation that constitutes a fundamental threat to obedient discipleship. Here, as in all other areas of Christian life and witness, there is a constant need for continual self-examination and for a posture of openness before the God of the Scriptures.

MOVING TOWARD THE SPECIFIC

If the preaching of the word will usually relate to political matters by attempting to provide the people of God with principles and guidelines to aid them in their own decision-making, what other steps will be necessary to aid Christians in dealing with concrete political matters? A helpful suggestion has recently been offered by Henry Pietersma:

> Couldn't the sermon, understood as authoritative word addressed to us, be followed by dialogue to which the whole congregation, in particular experts, contribute? In the case under discussion, for example, a sermon particularly concerned with political issues would end in a discussion in which everybody takes part. When available, Christian political scientists, sociologists, and economists should by all means contribute to such an opinion-forming dialogue. Such a dialogue need not lead to unanimity as to what particular course is to be followed in politics. But as I see it, its usefulness does not depend on that. And it would rid us of the need for political sermons. The preached gospel would become as concrete as life itself, but authoritative delivery of a message would be only part of this movement from the Bible to life ("Political Preaching," *The Reformed Journal,* September 1972, pp. 6-7).

An important point in this suggestion is that the dialogue over our concrete responses of obedience to the word need not result in unanimity. The unity of the Christian community resides in its common openness to the word, its common willingness to respond obediently to that word, and its common commitment to a free, open, and mutually accepting struggle together before the word. Thus, even where it cannot be realistically expected that all will agree as to what concrete courses of action to follow, Christians must be willing to examine together their attitudes, actions,

83

and policies with the spirit of openness expressed by the Psalmist: "Search me, O God, and know my heart! Try me and know my thoughts! And see if there be any wicked way in me, and lead me in the way everlasting" (Psalm 139:23-24).

The degree to which the pulpit may issue declarations on political matters, then, is not a matter that can be decided by appeal to a simple formula. There are times when a very clear and specific word of pastoral guidance may be required; there are other times, however, when the guidance will have to be of a more general sort. Much the same can be said of the other ways by which the church can officially "take stands." But at the very least, those who engage in the teaching and pastoral ministries of the institutional church must encourage the people of God to seek the way of political obedience. This can be done by supporting communal dialogue and shared struggle on these issues among Christians. There is no reason, for example, why the institutional church ought not to sponsor political workshops and caucuses to deal even more concretely with political matters than the sort of "dialogue-after-sermon" suggested above.

In sum, the institutional church, through the preaching and teaching which are central to its calling, can help to promote sensitivity to matters of political obedience among Christians in general; and it can foster a climate of dialogue and mutual accountability among those Christians who are engaged in political activity. Furthermore, it can and must continue to remind all Christians concerning their political involvement—whether that be exercised through voting, holding public office, or participating in groups of Christians organized for action in areas of politics, labor, etc.—that all of their opinions, tactics, ideologies and partisan commitments must be considered tentative in the light of loyalty to Jesus Christ.

Especially in this day when Christians are divided over how political obedience is to be exercised, it is important that dialogue be encouraged. Columnist Carl Rowan has often remarked that the struggle for equality among black people has been aided by action on many fronts—young blacks angrily denouncing "the system," individuals calmly working "within the system," charismatic leaders publicly proclaiming a vision of a society characterized by justice and equality—all of which has seemed to work together to create a climate for change that no single approach could hope to accomplish. If the institutional church can promote an atmosphere in which the tactical diversity of Christians in politics can be undergirded by a common concern for Christian obedience and a commitment to sharing together the ways different persons seek to be faithful disciples, we can have a legitimate hope that those efforts will be more effectively coordinated into a harmonious showing forth of the glory of God.

THE ROLE OF DIALOGUE

In discussing strategies for political evangelism we have placed great emphasis on the role of dialogue within the Christian community. In doing so, it may be fairly argued, we have not answered the "What shall we do?" question in any exhaustive way. In the next chapter we shall deal with some of the tensions that characterize the Christian's activities in the world under present conditions, in order to give further guidance for the formation of strategies for political evangelism.

But it must be admitted outright that particular

strategies can finally be formed only in the ongoing struggles of the people of God seeking to be politically obedient. This line of thinking, of course, borders on the recommendation of "All talk, no action." But it must also be admitted that twentieth-century Christians have done very little talking together on these things with any sense of communal dialogue, responsibility, and accountability. If "All talk, no action" is a danger, so are "All action, no talk" and "No talk, no action." If a commitment to dialogue and an attempt to foster and structure it within the Christian community can be seen as a necessary preparation for faithful political discipleship, we may begin to know God's blessing on our attempts at political evangelism.

Finally, dialogue can also encourage those inclined to engage in a "radical" sort of political evangelism to maintain the charity and humility proper in a disciple of Jesus Christ. Those who would stimulate the Body of Christ to wrestle seriously with justice, peace, and political discipleship must do so with a genuine concern to build up the people of God in love. This must be carried out, not by judgmental denunciation, but rather by sharing with other Christians a concern to live in full obedience to Jesus Christ as Lord, not only over our sexual activities, our personal habits, our church attendance, and our scientific theorizing, but also over our votes, our economic practices, and our trigger fingers.

POLITICAL EVANGELISM: THE HOPE AND THE TENSIONS

"Then he showed me the river of the water of life, bright as crystal, flowing from the throne of God and of the Lamb through the middle of the street of the city; also, on either side of the river, the tree of life with its twelve kinds of fruit, yielding its fruit each month; and the leaves of the tree were for the healing of the nations." *Revelation 22:1-2*

LET US SUMMARIZE BRIEFLY the main points of our discussion to this point.

The *scope* of the evangelistic activity of the people of God must include the presentation of the *fulness* of the power of the gospel as it confronts the cosmic presence of sin in the created order. *Political* evangelism, then, is one important aspect of this overall task of evangelism. The *primary agent* of evangelism is *God,* who has revealed his purposes for mankind in the reconciling work of Jesus Christ. The means by which God is accomplishing his redemptive purposes in the world, and is preparing the world for the full manifestation of his Kingdom at the return of Christ, is the presence of a *people* in the world. God's people are called by his sovereign mercy to *proclaim and demonstrate* through diverse means the marvels of his grace, which is a liberating force for all spheres, including the political sphere. The *base* for our evangelistic activity, the context out of which that activity must flow, is our life together, the building up of our *community* as the people of God on earth.

As we near the conclusion of our discussion, several things must yet be emphasized about the way in which our communal life together must relate to the work of political evangelism in the world, and the tensions of which we must be aware as we carry out that work.

CREDENTIALS AND MOTIVATION

Christian political witness must be firmly rooted in our individual experiences of life together as the people of God. Two things must be stressed here. First, our political witness must be rooted in our individual experiences. The community of the people of God is to be made up of those who have known in a personal way the radical power of the gospel. Take a concrete example. The individual Christian can speak confidently of the liberating power of the cross of Christ to bring an end to wars and rumors of wars among the nations. Why? Only because he knows the gospel as a power that has liberated him from his own *personal* wars. Only because he has prayed the prayer:

> *Just as I am, though tossed about*
> *With many a conflict, many a doubt,*
> *Fightings and fears, within, without,*
> *O Lamb of God, I come, I come.*

And, having approached the cross of Christ with that prayer, he has received the gift of peace.

Second, once we have experienced this personal liberation, it is important that our personal experiences of peace with God lead to reconciliation with others whom God has redeemed. "And this is his commandment, that we should believe in the name of his Son Jesus Christ and love one another" (I John 3:23). As the people of God we can speak together to the world of the possibility of genuine reconciliation and justice because we have begun to know in our life together the radical implications of the confession that "God was in Christ reconciling the world to himself" (II Corinthians 5:19).

But the reality of reconciliation and peace among

the people of God does not only provide us with the credentials for political witness, it is also our motivation and inspiration. As those who have experienced healing in our life together, we cannot be content in the knowledge that there is brokenness and suffering in the world. As those who regularly experience in our communal sacramental life the mercies of God toward helpless children we cannot remain silent before the spectacle of tiny napalmed bodies. As those who have cried out in gratitude:

> Forbid it, Lord, that I should boast
> Save in the death of Christ my God,
> All the vain things that charm me most,
> I sacrifice them through his blood,

we cannot be lulled into complacency by appeals to "national honor." As those who know the new life in which "there is neither Jew nor Greek, there is neither slave nor free, there is neither male nor female" (Galatians 3:28), we can only experience pain when we observe prejudiced and oppressive patterns of human association.

REALISM AND IDEALISM

Any Christian who expresses an interest in political and social change will sooner or later be reminded of the need to be "realistic." Such reminders are usually meant to point to the selfishness, even the wickedness, of men and the grave difficulties involved in promoting justice and peace. These reminders ought to be heeded. A political activism carried on in view of the cross of Jesus Christ cannot help being sensitive to the depravity of mankind, and to the pervasive human tendency to call good evil and evil good.

91

But the Christian must also act in the light of God's miraculous power, which is revealed in the resurrection, as well as in the cross, of Christ. From this perspective, being realistic means taking into account the fact that man's sinfulness does not speak the final word about human nature and destiny. We must not make the mistake of those early disciples who could not see beyond the scoffing crowd at Golgotha. In the light of the open tomb the disciples' pessimism was revealed as *unrealistic*. For the Christian, it is realistic to hope for resurrections after crucifixions. The Christian community must live in the constant realization that what the world calls idealism is often God's realism.

The Christian's political hope, then, must be firmly based on what God has accomplished and promised in Jesus Christ. In the early 1960s large numbers of sincere and dedicated young people, many of whom would not describe themselves as Christian believers, courageously committed themselves to nonviolent witnessing for the cause of justice and peace. Many of them were beaten and jailed. Some lost their lives. It was their conviction that their idealistic witness could bring about social and political improvement. These young people gave expression to their commitment and hope in these words: "Deep in my heart, I do believe, We shall overcome someday."

Since then many of these young people have lost that conviction. They have become cynical and embittered. From a Christian point of view, this should not be surprising. A hope based on mere conviction or feeling cannot long be sustained. The Christian's social-political hope goes deeper than this. The Christian's belief that "we shall overcome" is firmly rooted in his experience of the objective person and work of Jesus Christ. The hope of victory that the Christian cherishes was promised when sin entered into the world (Genesis 3:15); it was accomplished in principle by the one who, having suffered as we have suffered, said, "In the world you have tribulation, but be of good cheer, I have overcome the world" (John 16:33); and it will be fully accomplished in that future event envisioned by the Apostle of Patmos: "They will make war on the Lamb, and the Lamb will conquer them, for he is Lord of lords and King of kings, and those with him are called and chosen and faithful" (Revelation 17:14).

The Christian's hope is accompanied by the realization that the final victory is one God will bring about. The Scriptures promise that our acts of faithfulness relate to that final victory, but because we cannot always understand how, we must carry on, hoping that God will bless our efforts in such a way that they will relate to the final victory. The Christian is assured that his acts of obedience count for the coming of the Kingdom; but he cannot expect that they will count in accordance with the standards of success the world uses. Missionaries have spent entire lifetimes in Arab countries performing acts of mercy without ever seeing a person converted to Christianity. Yet in Christian terms their efforts count for the coming of the Kingdom of Jesus Christ. Similarly, the activities we pursue out of obedience to the political lordship of Christ count for the coming of his Kingdom.

Our efforts count, first of all, as evidence of the presence of the Kingdom of God among men. This is part of the "showing forth" activity of God's people. Second, our words and deeds count as invitations to others to submit to the lordship of Christ. Third, they are also, in a mysterious sense, ways in which we serve as agents of the Kingdom. This is the aspect indicated in the words of the hymn:

For not with swords' loud clashing,
Nor roll of stirring drums;
With deeds of love and mercy,
The heav'nly kingdom comes.

What now remains mysterious will become evident when the final victory is won—that our faithful deeds of love, our witness to the power of the gospel, have been ways in which we acted as *agents* of the Kingdom. Look again at the words quoted above from Revelation 17. The reference is not only to Christ's future victory, but also to the contributions of those who have spoken and acted in his name: "The Lamb will conquer them . . . and those with him are called and chosen and faithful."

PLURALISM AND POLITICAL EVANGELISM

Richard Hofstadter characterizes two very different political attitudes by this contrast:

> The political intelligence of our time . . . accepts conflict as a central and enduring reality and understands human society as a form of equipoise based upon the continuing process of compromise. It shuns ultimate showdowns and looks upon the ideal of total partisan victory as unattainable, as merely another variety of threat to the kind of balance with which it is familiar. It is sensitive to nuances and sees things in degrees. It is essentially relativist and skeptical, but at the same time circumspect and humane.
>
> The fundamentalist mind will have nothing to do with all this: it is essentially Manichean; it looks upon the world as an arena for conflict between absolute good and absolute evil, and accordingly it scorns compromise (who could compromise with Satan?) and can tolerate no ambiguities (*Anti-Intellectualism in American Life*, Vintage Books, 1962, pp. 134-135).

It is difficult to identify with either of the "minds" described here by Hofstadter, for there is something to accept and something to reject in each of them. Hofstadter's "fundamentalist" is wrong in seeing clear political choices as between absolute goods and absolute evils. The continuing influence of sin on the activities of the redeemed, as well as regular manifestations of "common grace" in the efforts of the unregenerate, make it impossible to see things in terms of such a "Manichean" scenario. But this is not to deny that the political sphere is one in which the forces of good and evil are in conflict; it is only to point out that those forces work under many guises, and sometimes infiltrate the same caucuses.

It is in this latter area that we must fault what Hofstadter calls "the political intelligence of our time," which, while rightly stressing the role of flexibility and tolerance in the political sphere, has often moved beyond that stress to a sheer relativism that replaces a plausible democratic principle—every man has a right to his own opinion—with an heretical one—every man is right in his own opinion.

Given a concern to avoid either of these extremes, the most plausible political framework for Christians to advocate and support is that of a pluralistic society. (For a detailed discussion of the issues involved here see Nicholas Wolterstorff's *Religion and the Schools*, Eerdmans, 1966.) This involves a commitment by Christians to a society governed by a posture of impartiality toward persons and groups whose pursuits and life-styles reflect a diversity of fundamental commitments.

Such a social and political framework is attractive from a Christian point of view for two reasons. First, the Body of Christ must advocate social and govern-

95

mental structures for the larger human community in which it is possible for the church to be itself, to be a community of people seeking to be obedient to the lordship of Jesus Christ. The people of God must seek the freedom to exercise this obedience in all dimensions of its life: education, labor, economics, and the like. If, for example, some Christians see the maintenance of a system of Christian elementary and secondary schools and colleges as the best way to pursue this obedience in the field of education, they will have the freedom to do so without unnecessary penalties. Or, if a Christian cannot participate in a given military project, or in *any* military activity, with a clear sense of obedience to Christ, he should be granted the legal right to refrain from such an engagement.

Second, a Christian will not only seek this freedom for himself. He will also want to advocate structures in which persons and groups with differing perspectives and loyalties are free to live out their commitments. Christians should not wish for the coercive imposition of Christian patterns of behavior on those who do not freely choose to serve the Lord; for God desires not grudging sacrifice but a heart of mercy. To use an analogy from sports, Christians should advocate a society in which many different basic commitments interact and whose government adopts the attitude of a referee, who sees to it that the competition is carried on fairly, and not the attitude of the coach, who is attempting to aid and cheer on one of the competing parties.

This raises important questions, to which we must be sensitive. When Christians advocate policies that promote justice and peace, are they not attempting to impose on others patterns that Christians see as rooted in a biblical perspective? Have we not insisted that the

Christian view of justice and peace is inseparably bound up in the experience of reconciliation and healing in the life of the people of God? Furthermore, are the sorts of policies of peace and justice possible in a pluralistic society not empty and fragmentary apart from the full, redemptive transformation that can only come by saving grace?

Several things must be pointed out in response to these questions. First, the Christian will be motivated to speak out against injustice and suffering simply because of the pain that he feels when, as one who has experienced reconciliation and healing, he is confronted by brokenness and oppression. Second, the very existence of a pluralistic society is based on a common commitment to justice and peace, even if some parties to the "social contract" are so committed only grudgingly and for selfish reasons. In such a social context the Christian community must assume the obligation to advocate the rights of all men to peace and justice; it must act as an agent that attempts to sensitize all citizens to human suffering and need wherever it exists.

Third, it must be acknowledged that Christians must often commit themselves to policies that from a biblical point of view will bring about only a fragmentary justice and peace. But such commitments are legitimate if we view them not as the end but the beginning of our Christian witness. Bishop Stephen Neill has made an interesting comment on the possibilities for dialogue between Christians and Buddhists which we can apply to our present concerns:

> The Buddhist ideal is that of passionless benevolence. The Christian ideal is that of compassion. When argument has done its best, we must perhaps leave the two ideals face to face. We can only ask our Buddhist friend to look

long and earnestly on the Cross of Christ, and to ask himself whether, beyond the peace of the Buddha, there may not be another dimension of peace to the attainment of which there is no way other than the Way of the Cross (*Christian Faith and Other Faiths,* Oxford University Press, 1961, p. 124).

Similarly, while the Christian attempts to promote a fragmentary peace and justice in the secular arena, he must do so with the assurance that the only truly satisfying justice and peace is that found by submission to the lordship of Jesus Christ. As he identifies with the needs of the suffering and the oppressed he must also seek the opportunity to point beyond the partial and fleeting peace and justice the world occasionally affords to the cross of Jesus Christ, which offers to men "the peace which passes human understanding."

FAITHFULNESS AND FLEXIBILITY

Political evangelism must be carried on in the awareness of the tensions of the present age. The victorious death and resurrection of Jesus Christ have broken and sealed the doom of Satan's rule. But the fulness of the power of the Kingdom of Christ is not yet present. To borrow a thought from Oscar Cullmann (and others), we are poised between the "no longer" of the rule of Satan and the "not yet" of the fulness of the Kingdom. It is not always easy to know what we are to do by way of obedient discipleship in such a situation. It is clear that we cannot simply act as if the end time is already here; on the other hand we cannot merely live out a series of concessions to the presence of sin. As G. C. Berkouwer puts it:

The church ... must be careful not to draw a direct conclusion from the triumph of Christ to its own perfection, possible or real. On the other hand, it must not, in an effort to ward off any tendencies to perfectionism, elevate the "not yet" to the status of norm in its own existence (*The Return of Christ*, Eerdmans, 1972, p. 138).

Henry Pietersma has suggested that the "unity of the Christian life" must be sought, in the present age, in terms of living in tension between acceptance and dissociation. Insofar as the Christian already participates in the new life made possible in Jesus Christ, he must detach himself from the sinful world. But insofar as he is not yet totally sanctified and still participates in the sinful order, his attitudes must be characterized by the realism and patience that come from an honest acceptance of his position in the history of redemption. Within this framework,

> the Christian life certainly has a kind of unity that it is important to emphasize. The old and the new are not neutral to one another. It is a unity in which acceptance of the old is tempered by detachment or dissociation as a result of our faith in the new. It is perfectly true that we have to obey Christ in all that we do or think. But total commitment to Christ involves precisely acceptance as well as dissociation. The unity of the Christian life involves a tension that Christians should never cease to feel ("The Unity of the Christian Life," *Reformed Journal*, July-August 1971, p. 15).   *164638*

Arthur Gish recognizes the need to act in the awareness of this sort of tension when he distinguishes between two kinds of compromise:

> It is one thing to talk of compromise in the sense of flexibility and cooperation, a willingness to live ambiguities of life, to be aware of our questionable motives and imperfect actions, to reject dogmatism; and it is quite another thing to talk of selling out, retreating, being less than faithful, basing decisions on expediency rather than on faithfulness to one's commitment (*The New Left and Christian Radicalism*, Eerdmans, 1970, p. 95).

The difficulty, of course, is knowing in which sort of compromise one is engaging at a given moment. How does one decide whether what he is doing is a case of being flexible or one of selling out? There is no simple formula for deciding. The kind of flexibility that must characterize Christian political attitudes and strategies is not based ultimately on an ideology, a set of rules, or some mechanical guide to decision-making. There are times when flexibility will require that the Christian must work for gradual change, laboring patiently within the system. There are other times when faithfulness to the demands of the gospel will require protest, judgment, and a refusal to walk the way of expediency. To decide what is required in a given situation will often be difficult. In such times the Christian has no other recourse but to seek the will of God through prayer, to search the Scriptures, and to struggle within the context of the community of the people of God to know his leading. Ultimately, the hope for guidance in Christian discipleship rests on a trust in the promises of God that he will provide the gift of discernment under the supervision of his Spirit.

THE TENSIONS OF DISCIPLESHIP

No doubt some readers will be dissatisfied with the flavor of this discussion. They may find in it overtones of "situationism." Be that as it may, it must be pointed out that while we have stressed the need for struggle in a way seldom acknowledged by many who typically appeal to rules and formulas, we have also insisted that the struggle must be one which seeks obedience to the word of God. The kind of guidance the Christian must seek is not the sort that normally comes through mystical intuitions or visions, nor is it the kind that makes simple deductions or applications from Scripture or theology. It is the kind that emerges out of the disciplined life of obedience, one that includes a concern for sound theology and a posture of openness to the teaching ministry of the church. The way of discipleship is, so to speak, "of a piece." The Christian may not merely hope that when the time of decision and crisis comes he will receive instant guidance; his life must be a continual preparation for such a time, so that when he faces the situation the prayer and study and dialogue that have characterized his daily walk will have developed his understanding and sensitivity to the point that he can discern the requirements of obedience.

Other readers will criticize this present discussion as characterized by endless qualification and tentativeness. But there need be no apologies offered for stressing the tensions that characterize the task of political evangelism. Undoubtedly there are dangers inherent in emphasizing the ambiguities of the present age. But they are no greater than the dangers that lie in wait for those who assume an "ideological" posture. Whichever path we take—refusal to participate in political activity or political activism or cautious involvement—the danger of idolatrous attachment is always present. The human race is notoriously capable of self-deception; and in this Christians are all too human. The only truly "radical" Christianity is that which flows out of a posture of radical openness before our Lord; and this means we have to be willing to place our self-devised formulas, ideologies, even our peculiar packagings of orthodoxy—whether it be in terms of "spiritual laws," "sphere-laws," "social gospel" or whatever else—for critical scrutiny, judgment, and sanctification under his gaze.

Not only political evangelism, but the Christian life in general, must be pursued in the face of tensions. We can allow ourselves to be incapacitated by them, or we can seek to escape them by taking refuge in manipulative techniques and party lines, or we can respond to them by creatively struggling to know the mind of Christ. For those who are willing to take that struggle upon themselves, there is the promise that can bring hope even in the midst of the tensions:

> Fear not, for I am with you, be not dismayed, for I am your God; I will strengthen you, I will help you, I will uphold you with my victorious right hand (Isaiah 41:10).

8

A CONCLUDING MEDITATION

"He is the image of the invisible God, the first-born of all creation; for in him all things were created, in heaven and on earth, visible and invisible, whether thrones or dominions or principalities or authorities—all things were created through him and for him. He is before all things, and in him all things hold together. He is the head of the body, the church; he is the beginning, the first-born from the dead, that in everything he might be pre-eminent. For in him all the fulness of God was pleased to dwell, and through him to reconcile to himself all things, whether on earth or in heaven, making peace by the blood of his cross."

Colossians 1:15-20

THROUGHOUT HISTORY the people of God have been tempted to fall into idolatrous patterns and pay homage to finite powers in such a way that those powers rival the power of God. In the Old Testament Israel continually tried to find some legitimate role for the gods of her neighbors. In the Colossian church, to whom Paul wrote the words at the head of this chapter, some Christians were attempting—perhaps under the influence of a gnosticizing Judaism—to placate a plurality of "invisible powers" in a way that dishonored the gospel. This has also been true of recent Christianity. Even where there has been great sensitivity to the possibilities for idolatry and unfaithfulness in the areas of cultural pursuits, personal habits, and worldly wisdom, there have often been too-easy truces declared between the household of faith and the citadels of political power.

To counter the threat of idolatry—political or otherwise—that continues in the New Testament church, Paul points to the supreme power of Jesus Christ, emphasizing two aspects of it. First, he points to the creating and sustaining power of God in Christ. The Son of God is the source of all things, both visible and invisible. Whatever we reckon with—"thrones or dominions or principalities or·authorities"—has its source and being in the creative work of Jesus Christ, and "in him all things hold together."

But these thoughts as such provide little personal comfort and guidance. A theology of politics based solely on the themes of creation and providence cannot get us very far. The Christian who lives under the rule of a power-mad dictator can, on one level, take comfort in the knowledge that his faithfulness can be exercised without ultimately fearing that dictator's power, and he can carry on in the trust that his enemy is sustained by the very power of Jesus Christ. But important questions still remain. How shall he exercise his faithfulness? How shall he carry on, possessing, as he does, a trust in the ultimacy of the creating and sustaining power of God?

The comfort provided by our belief in God's creating and sustaining work is of a rather abstract sort. It assures us that whatever happens, whatever the power balance in human relations may seem to be at a given moment, God is nonetheless in control, and he is faithfully working out his good purposes among men. And abstract though it be, there will be times when we must desperately seek comfort from our faith in God's ultimate control over human affairs. But this comfort may never be legitimately gained simply by resigning ourselves to the fact that his purposes are being worked out. When Jeremiah heard a frightening commotion in the north country and foresaw the doom of Judah he confessed, "I know, O Lord, that the way of man is not in himself, that it is not in man who walks to direct his steps." But he did not stop there. He quickly added: "*Correct* me, O Lord . . . " (Jeremiah 10:23-24). Our comfort in God's sovereign purposes in history must be intimately related to the active *trust* with which we seek to do his will. Only when our faith in providence is a feature of our lives of obedience to the revealed will of the God of providence can we rightly allow that faith to be applied to our comfort.

Thus, like Jeremiah, the Apostle cannot stop with a hymn to the creating and sustaining power of Jesus Christ in the universe. He also offers a prescription for the "Correct me" plea: "He is the head of the body, the church." Here Paul speaks of the second aspect of the supreme power of Jesus Christ, pointing to the redemptive and reconciling power of God. The New English Bible adds a word that brings out the drama of this transition sentence: "He is, *moreover,* the head of the body, the church."

To grow in the Christian life we must continually hear a "moreover" concerning the person and work of Jesus Christ. When we are so impressed by his role as judge that we would crumble to the ground before him, as John did on Patmos, when he beheld Christ as one whose "eyes were like a flame of fire," we must hear the "Fear not" that reminds us that he is, *moreover,* the one who bore our sins in his own body. When we are tempted to rest contentedly in the fellowship of his redeemed people, we must be reminded that he is, *moreover,* the one who calls us to cast our lot with the poor and the outcasts. When we are so weighed down by the burdens of social injustice and oppression that we have thoughts for little else, we must hear that he is, *moreover,* the one who bids us come to the place where we can find rest for our souls.

Christ is the creator and sustainer of all things. "He is—moreover—the head of the body, the church." His redemptive and reconciling activities do reach, of course, beyond the bounds of the church. But as we look and reflect on the apparent chaos and fragmentation of the world around us, it is not easy to see his power at work. It is not easy to see him at work amid the hatred of race against race. It is not easy to hear his voice among the wailing of sirens and the bursting of bombs and the angry demands for "liberation."

In some mysterious way, incomprehensible to us, he is there, of course: "in him all things hold together." But how he is in these things, working out his good purposes, is presently a mystery. It is so much a mystery that to confess that he is working in and through these events would be to mouth empty platitudes were it not often so desperately important that we believe in his creating and sustaining power. When we read Jeremiah's confession of faith in God's providence, we suspect that his voice quavered a bit when he said, "*I know,* O Lord, that the way of man is not in himself . . . "—much like the child who cries out in the dark, "You *are* there, Mommy, aren't you?"

But: "he is—moreover—the head of the body, the church." To realize the implications of this "moreover" is—Paul goes on to say—to understand "the mystery" (vs. 26). The mystery we have been discussing—the mystery of how the words we confess concerning the creating and sustaining power of God can be true—can be unraveled, at least partly, by the realization that "he is—moreover—the head of the body, the church." The answer to "the mystery hidden for ages and generations," the answer "now made manifest to his saints," is this: "Christ in you, the hope of glory."

"He is—moreover—the head of the body, the church . . . Christ in you, the hope of glory." Where is he, among the hatred and sirens and bombs and angry cries? Why can we not see his glory in these things? How *is* he preeminent in these things? And do they, or will they, show forth his glory? Paul answers: Look at the church, it is there that we can experience the *hope* of glory.

God in Jesus Christ is working out his purposes in the world. It is not obvious that he is doing so. But he is. And he has not left us without a witness, without a sign, of the glory that will someday be revealed in and through all that he has done. For the work he is carrying on secretly and mysteriously throughout the created order, even in this present time, is of a piece with the work he is doing openly in "the body, the church." When, in the life together of the people of God, we see anger graciously transformed into love and acceptance, we have received a glimpse of the glory that will be revealed in the day when all creation will be transformed into a choir singing a hymn of love and joy. When in our life together we experience a reconciliation that creates such a trust and a sensitivity that it pains us to hear the sirens and bombs, we have received a glimpse of the glory that will be revealed when men will no longer fashion weapons of manipulation and destruction. When in the "political" life of the church we are freed for service and self-sacrifice, we have experienced something of the Kingdom of Jesus Christ that will someday cover all the earth.

"He is—moreover—the head of the body, the church." Jesus Christ is not only the one who presently and mysteriously holds all things together; he is also the one who invites us into fellowship with himself. He calls us to eat and drink with him, to share in the revelation of the "mystery" that had been hidden heretofore.

It is no mere arbitrary stipulation on God's part that "outside of the church there is no salvation." God calls us to the community in which he is restoring the fellowship for which man was created. It is in that community, of which Jesus is head, where we can find healing and wholeness. Political evangelism must begin

109

there, and it must continually draw on the strength to be found in the sanctified weakness that resides there. It is there that the Lord of politics gathers his people and teaches them the lessons that point to the glory, even the *political* glory, that is yet to come.

But he does not only call us to the life together that is to be found in his body, the church. Having brought us to the place where he is publicly and openly doing his work of redemption and reconciliation, he sends us forth into the world, where he is secretly and mysteriously working out his purposes. And this is what he tells us to do, in the words of Peter: we must "declare the wonderful deeds of him who called you out of darkness into his marvelous light." Having been shown the answer to the mystery, we then become the link between the work that he is doing in the church and the unifying task he is mysteriously working out in the entire created order.

It is because we have known his power in the church that we can proclaim his power in the world. Having been healed, we are sent to do a healing work among men. As those who have known the benefits of his sacrifice, we can offer ourselves as living sacrifices for the mission of his church.

From the community that exists under his direct authority, he sends us forth to confront the "thrones or dominions or principalities or authorities" he has created, which are held together by him. This confrontation must not result in idolatrous submission on our part, nor does it have to lead us to react in anarchistic rebellion; for "in *him* all things hold together."

How shall we confront, even serve, the powers that he has ordained? We are not left alone to act without guidance. For the one who has created those powers, and who holds them together, is the one who sends us forth to declare his marvelous works in their presence.

"He is before all things, and in him all things hold together. He is—moreover—the head of the body, the church."